Growth and Welfare
A New Policy for Britain

Growth
and Welfare
A New Policy for Britain

John Mills

Martin Robertson

First published in 1972 by
Martin Robertson & Company Ltd.,
17 Quick Street London N1 8HL

ISBN 0 85520 012 X

Set by Santype Limited (Coldtype Division) Salisbury and printed by The Pitman Press Bath.

Contents

Foreword
by Sir Roy Harrod

I am much pleased at having been asked to write a preface to this interesting and outstanding book. It is an orderly and systematic treatise set out in good logical order. Its author has a fine grasp of modern economics and especially of that part of it that is concerned with economic growth. The literature on this topic still remains weak. For some reason our leading economists do not seem to have got around and addressed their minds to developing theories in this area. It is perhaps a normal human tendency to fight shy of a new topic; on the other hand it ought to attract those of adventurous outlook. There is more scope for breaking new ground in this field than in other parts of economics. It is not only a question of tidying up or exploring by-paths. The main structure of growth economics has not yet been built.

Mr Mills' book should be a notable landmark in the development of this branch.

While it is with some enthusiasm that I write a preface commending it to economic thinkers, I feel a conscientious scruple that compels me to express dissent on certain matters. I hold that the author makes much too light of the evil of inflation. He says that 'it is argued that inflation leads to worsening distribution of income, and in particular that inflation hits those on fixed income, the poor and unsophisticated'. I am not convinced about the efficacy of his proposals for mitigating this evil. While I agree with the author that measures required to insure optimum growth must be given top priority, yet the prevention of inflation should have very high priority. If on rare occasions there is some trade-off between optimum growth and inflation, it is nonetheless possible that the evil of allowing inflation is greater than that of preventing growth from being as great as it ought to be. The main trouble in some advanced countries in recent years has been that the authorities have wrongly thought that measures designed to check growth would necessarily tend to mitigate inflation. This is quite wrong; Mr Mills understands this point very well.

My second point of disagreement concerns the measure to which he gives pride of place as the leading remedy for failures to achieve the various targets that he sets out. This is depreciation of the foreign exchange rate. My objection to this, first and foremost, is that by itself it is unneighbourly. One man's 'depreciation' is 'appreciation' for the other. In this field we have to look at matters from an international point of view. A measure should not be accepted simply because it is useful for a particular country; we must balance this against its demerits to other countries. If there is to be an exchange rate adjustment, there should be international consensus. We lack regular machinery for getting this; in this connection, the International Monetary Fund does not seem to be in full control, as was originally intended. But, underlying this, there is a much deeper trouble. There is no agreement among economists, whether theoretical or practical, about the underlying principles that should govern changes in exchange rates. Until this matter is sorted out, one should be very cautious about the use of this remedy. Incidentally, it is not a certain remedy for an external deficit; its remedial effect depends on the elasticities of supply and demand being sufficient. There was a striking case in recent years, that of Germany, in which an upward adjustment did not reduce its trade surplus.

Usually growth should be secured by domestic measures. The author's criticisms of a reliance on these depends rather on the authorities not having pursued them whole-heartedly than on their inadequacy to achieve the target of optimum growth. If in consequence of adequate measures an external deficit develops, then, and then only, is the time to have a look at an exchange depreciation to rectify matters. But it may not always be the right recipe; that depends on the circumstances of the case; in certain circumstances, direct import restriction may be better.

Finally, the author appears in his first page to me to be too despondent about the British performance since the war. During this period, I have travelled around the world a good deal, and my impression has been that England has been coming forward more quickly than other free market countries, except for Japan.

Even comparing her with the great United States, which takes the lead in the world in most of the respects with which we are concerned, there appear to me to be many areas in which English 'services' seem not only to be increasing more rapidly, but to be absolutely superior to the equivalent services in the U.S.A. I would cite shopping facilities, restaurant facilities, transport, communications, education. These areas cover quite a lot of the whole ground of 'services'.

Also great attention has been paid in England during this period to preserving or increasing amenities. It may be that the trouble taken in this area has been at some cost to the growth of the GNP. Economics should be concerned with human welfare, and the preservation or increase of amenities is just as important as an increase of marketable goods and services.

The GNP is a very important tool in the assessment of human welfare, but should not be relied on exclusively.

Acknowledgements

Far too many people have contributed in one way or another to what is in this book for it to be possible to name them all here. Certainly all those whose names appear in the notes to the text ought to be included in any comprehensive list, and I would like to thank everyone whose books and articles I read while the research for this book was being carried out. I hope that in all cases their ideas have been acknowledged in the notes so that any plagiarism is at least admitted.

However, there are certain people who have played such an important part in getting this book written that they must be thanked individually. Susan Squires compiled the reading list on which most of the research was based, and Catherine Winnett spent much of the summer of 1971 compiling statistics, checking facts and providing opinions, assisted by her husband. The mathematics was checked through by Mr Michael Milford, and its presentation improved as a result of a number of suggestions he made.

When the first draft was completed it was distributed to three people who have made a very great contribution to the published version. My former economics tutor, Professor John Black of Exeter University, not only produced a large number of written comments on the text, but also spent a considerable amount of time going through detailed points in an extended latter day tutorial. Sir Roy Harrod also contributed a great deal of detailed criticism in a series of letters and has been kind enough to agree to write a Foreword to the book. Mr Walter Eltis of Exeter College, Oxford, read through two drafts of the book and his help has been particularly important in drawing my attention to the challenges to the argument that may be forthcoming from conventional growth economics, and suggesting how these might be met. Dr Meghnad Desai, of the London School of Economics, was also of great assistance in resolving various mathematical points.

A number of people outside the academic world have commented especially on the more policy orientated sections of the book. In particular I should like to thank Mr Peter Moyes of The M.E.L. Equipment Company, Mr Terry Pitt from the Labour Party Research Department, and Mr Lawrence Whitty of the Economic Department of the T.U.C.

No list of acknowledgements would be complete without mentioning all those people whose lives have been disorganised to a greater or lesser extent by the time it has taken me to get this book finished. In particular I should like to thank my wife and family, and my business colleagues for their tolerance and understanding, and especially my secretary, Jan, who never complains however much work she is given to do.

Finally, I must make the usual disclaimer about anyone mentioned in this list of acknowledgements being in any way responsible for what follows. It is most unfortunate that economists speak with such discordant voices, and I would like to think that this book might be of some help in narrowing down the disparity of opinions which economists put forward by rationalising some of the preconceptions upon which both their theories and prescriptions are based.

John Mills
March 1972

To
Barbara, Sarah, Caroline,
Elizabeth and Peter

Chapter I A Century of Relative Economic Decline

The performance of the British economy during the quarter century since the end of World War II, and indeed for many years before that, has been inferior to that attained in many other parts of the world. We are the only country in Northern Europe where unemployment is still a serious and persistent problem. Our rates of inflation are above average at least for the developed world. We suffer from chronic balance of payments problems which we have bought off only temporarily with massive deflation. Our rate of economic growth is just about the lowest in the whole world; most developed countries now enjoy a higher standard of living than ours, and most of those which are less developed are catching us up, some of them very rapidly. There can be few people who feel contented with this record, but there are many who regard it as inevitable. There are even more who are not very interested in economic matters and who turn their attention to other affairs.

The central contentions in this book are that the relatively poor economic performance achieved in Britain is exceedingly important but not inevitable. It is very important because almost every goal anyone of us has, whether personal, social or political, depends on a reasonably successful economic environment for its attainment. The contention that we could do very much better economically than we have done rests on the proposition that different policies, based on a new look at some areas of economic theory, would provide us with a very much better chance of being able to achieve at least most, if not all, the economic objectives which are generally held to be important.

Most people would agree that current economic theory does not offer a comprehensive solution to our present economic problems. The submission in this book is that these are two main reasons why this is the case. First, there are substantial areas of conflict involved in trying to achieve all accepted economic objectives at once, and there is no method available of deciding their relative importance. Is it worth having less economic growth if the result is less inflation? If so, how much growth should be sacrificed to achieve how much reduction in inflation? Is it worth increasing unemployment to safeguard the current parity of sterling? If so, how much unemployment is it reasonable to accept before the cost outweighs the benefit? These sorts of questions are very important and our first task will be to work out a systematic method of tackling them.

Armed with the results of this inquiry we can then move on to prescription and venture into the second area where current theory is deficient. This is in explaining what causes economic growth, and what can be done, which falls within the domain of practical policy, to achieve one rate of growth rather than another. If Britain's poor record is wholly attributable to premature maturity, or lack of the right physical resources, or a social structure that produces poor managers and bad salesmen, or all these factors and a host of others all totally beyond the power of the government to change, then no prescriptions are going to make the situation much better. However, there are other explanations. In the first place there is no particular reason for believing that we are especially disadvantaged compared with other countries by our physical environment, and our political and social legacy. Other countries have problems of this sort too, and there are some very striking areas where we have great advantages over most of the rest of the world. To cite only two, our labour force is better educated than nearly all others, and the levels of toleration and social cohesion in this country are certainly greater than in most other parts of the world. Secondly there is no doubt that a great deal, though not all, capital investment that can be undertaken is exceedingly productive, and there seems to be no good reason why investment undertaken in Japan should necessarily have a very high rate of return while the same investment undertaken in Britain should have a very low return. However, there is no doubt that the Japanese do get very much better results from their investment than we do although one might have thought that they had rather similar problems to ours. After all, Japan is an island, short of natural resources, highly populated and unable to supply more than a proportion of the foodstuffs it requires.

How do the Japanese do it? Is it the hand of fate that gives us a low rate of economic growth and them a high one, or is our pattern of investment worse than theirs, smaller in size and inadequately utilised when it is installed? Even if the cards are stacked up against us to some extent, it seems very unlikely that bad economic management has not got something to do with our predicament. If we can identify what the main areas of economic bad management are and substitute effective policies for ineffective ones *at least in the areas which are within our policy control*, might it not be possible to put our situation to rights? This is the second area where we shall concentrate our inquiries, and we shall find as our investigation is pursued that there is a great deal of evidence which suggests that our rate of growth is very much more determined by policy and less by immutable laws of nature than is currently accepted.

Both of the lines of inquiry proposed above, evaluation of the relative importance of different economic objectives, and investigating what produces one rate of economic growth rather than another, are comparatively new areas of interest for economists. Until the Second World War it was held to be the duty of the state, at least in Britain, to be the referee rather than a player, and active interventionist policies were not in favour. The problems of reconciling major competing objectives were therefore less acute. It was only towards the end of World War II that the government began to feel itself committed to a policy of maintaining full employment. After the war there came a spate of commitments to various targets by a succession of Chancellors of the Exchequer: various reiterations of a full employment target, expressed in terms of an average percentage of unemployment which was not to be exceeded (3% by Mr Gaitskell in 1950 for example): a balance of payments target, expressed in terms of a current surplus of so many millions (such as the £300 million put forward by Mr — now Lord — Butler in 1962, and the £450 million proposed by the Radcliffe Committee in 1959); a growth target (4% by Mr Maudling in 1964 and 3.8% in the National Plan of 1965) and a wage-increase or incomes policy target (by Sir Stafford Cripps in 1949; by Mr Selwyn Lloyd in 1962; by Mr Reginald Maudling in 1964 and Mr George Brown in 1965; by legislation in 1966).[1] It did not take long before all concerned discovered the extent to which attempts to improve performance in any one of these areas tended to depress the achievements in nearly all the others.

While economic growth has nearly always been considered desirable, it was not regarded as being much within the competence of the government to achieve one rate of growth rather than another until after the Second World War, and serious public interest in the subject only arose towards the end of the 1950's when it became apparent that Britain was doing very poorly compared with other countries. Interest in growth was spurred on by the urgent needs of poor countries to which it was felt this country ought to contribute; by Cold War considerations which concerned not only military matters but also the realisation that the economic achievements of the Soviet bloc were rivalling those in the West and particularly in Britain; and by a general realisation that without adequate economic resources a great number of social and political objectives were not going to be achieved. It would be pleasant to record that as a result there was an increase in our growth rate; unhappily, despite the considerable increase in investment which took place in the 1960's both relatively and absolutely, our growth rate did not increase at all. One of the main objectives in this book is to explain why this happened, and to put forward policy proposals which should have a much higher chance of being successful, based on a rather different theoretical explanation as to what produces faster or slower rates of growth than is usually accepted.

Economic Growth and Policy Conflicts

Let us now turn to the question of policy conflicts in a little more detail. What are the main objectives of economic policy as seen at present? The following have been put forward:
- economic growth
- balance of payments in surplus or at least in equilibrium
- stable currency — not too much inflation
- full employment
- freedom of choice
- productive efficiency
- high current standard of living
- fixed exchange rates
- greater equality of wealth and income

Of these objectives there is almost universal agreement about the desirability of the first four, despite the difficulties in reconciling conflicts between them. The next three objectives are also accepted by nearly everyone, but since they are all subsidiary to the first four they will not be dealt with as separate policy goals though we shall see how they could be achieved as the analysis in this book develops. Although when one looks back over the 1960's it might seem as though fixed exchange rates were regarded as the most important objective of all, many people doubted even then whether they really did represent a desirable policy goal. In our analysis we shall go further and question whether even the present proposals for introducing a little more flexibility could not be radically altered to the general advantage. Finally we have the question of income and wealth distribution, perhaps the most overtly political of all our objectives, and therefore one on which universal agreement is not to be expected. For this reason the procedure adopted is to note the effects of other policies on income and wealth distribution, but to treat reductions in these distributions as being more in the domain of politics than economics.

Considering that the conflict between at least the main four commonly agreed objectives has been well known for some time it seems pertinent to ask why so little has in fact been done to work out priorities in a systematic fashion, particularly for the U.K., where the conflicts have turned out to be especially severe. This is a question which seems to have several answers.

In the first place it took time for people to realise how serious and long lasting these conflicts were going to be. The early post World War II success of British economic policies was impressive both in relation to the interwar period, and to most other countries which had suffered far more severely during the hostilities than the U.K. These successes were particularly striking in view of the liquidation of financial assets which had been necessary to raise money for supplies during the war, combined with the large debts which had been run up with various sterling area countries in the course of obtaining more supplies on credit. As the immediate postwar period receded into the past two other factors greatly assisted the British economy, thus making awkward choices less immediately necessary. One was the steady reduction in military expenditure from 11.1% of National Income in 1953 to 7.1% in 1960,[2] after its peak during the Korean War. The other was the very marked improvement in Britain's terms of trade, especially as regards many of our raw materials, during the fifties — 13% during period 1951-53 and a further 14%[3] in the late fifties. These two substantial once-and-for-all benefits masked the seriousness of the problems Britain was facing until the early sixties, when Reginald Maudling's attempt to reflate Britain out of recession in 1964 finally brought home to everyone, not least the new Labour Government, just how serious the position was. Indeed the record of Britain in the sixties and early seventies was such that compared to almost everywhere else in the developed world we were not only failing to achieve all the objectives which everyone agreed were desirable, but we were barely achieving any of them at all. Maudling's attempt to achieve faster growth led to a balance of payments crisis with which the Labour government struggled for the next six years. The objective of stable exchange rates was sacrificed to devaluation in 1967 accompanied by massive deflation. Over the period 1960-69 our rate of growth was only just over half the average for all O.E.C.D. countries, 3.0% as against 5.0%[4], and at the end of the decade unemployment was in an apparently inexorable upward spiral. By early 1972 we were in a situation where the rate of inflation was some 10% p.a., unemployment was over the million mark, growth was still very low by international standards, and the balance of payments situation was steadily deteriorating again. Gone too was the credibility of the theories that other countries were catching us up because they started off at a lower level; many of them were rapidly passing us in terms of output per head, Germany in the early sixties followed by France, Denmark, Norway and the Benelux countries by the end of the decade.[5]

If the seriousness of the conflict between the various policy goals was generally underestimated until well into the sixties, during this decade they became something of a national obsession. When the dire nature of our predicament was made manifest it also unfortunately became apparent that there was no body of economic theory available to provide solutions. In consequence it was not surprising to find a policy vacuum with the Chancellor claiming he was merely 'touching the tiller', when in fact he had no more idea than anyone else where the ship was supposed to be going. It was particularly unfortunate that there was no economic analysis explaining how to achieve economic growth, or why Britain's record was so poor. While at least there was a substantial corpus of reasonably well developed prescriptive theory on inflation, the balance of payments and unemployment, there simply was no comparable theory on growth. The consequences were all too obvious. Whenever there was a serious conflict of objectives growth was always relegated to the bottom of the list of priorities, and policies of deflation, the very antithesis of growth, were adopted. Economic growth theory has of course been the object of academic study but the line of development pursued has been mostly concerned with abstract models which are difficult to relate back to the real world, and which therefore have very little prescriptive content. Perhaps two quotations from recognised experts in the field will bring home the flavour of their endeavours better than any description:

> "It is partly a measure of the complexity of economic growth that the phenomenon of growth should remain, after three decades of intensive intellectual study, such an enigma. It is, however, also a reflection of our sense of values, particularly of the preoccupation with brain twisters. Part of the difficulty arises undoubtedly from the fact that the selection of topics for work in growth economics is guided much more by logical curiosity than by taste for relevance. The character of the subject owes much to this fact."
> (*Growth Economics* by Amartya Sen, Penguin Modern Econqmics Readings 1970, p 33)

> "Dynamic Welfare Economics ought, in principle, to face all the standard difficulties of Static Welfare Economics. Interpersonal comparison, increasing returns, external economies — the lions in the path of static theory — all remain with us. It is scarcely to be expected that they will be more tractable when they are taken in a dynamic setting. A general dynamic theory, which fits all these things into their places, is quite out of reach. It will certainly not be offered here. We shall have to content ourselves with something much simpler."
> (*Capital and Growth* by John Hicks, Oxford University Press 1965, pp 201/202)

In sum, the failure of economic growth theory to put forward any coherent justification for one rate of growth as against another, or to explain how any rate of growth is to be achieved, has meant that the significance of economic growth as an attainable policy objective has never really been appreciated.

It also seems that part of the reason for our failure to break out of our dismal economic predicament is a widespread fatalistic feeling that the situation is hopeless and beyond rational control. Unfortunately, this sentiment has manifested itself through many sections of British society over the last few years. In the academic and journalistic world our economic failure have been blamed on everything from historic trends to a lack of labour available to more from the agricultural sector to more productive employment, from an overvalued exchange rate which could not be altered to an undesirable pattern of foreign trade, the implication being that our economic circumstances were beyond policy control and our failures inevitable. Politicians and civil servants, left to cope with the practical problems of what to do next without much theoretical guidance, have understandably chased all the commonly accepted objectives at once. Having consistently failed to achieve any of them, and at a loss as to where to turn next, many of them have seized with a near hysterical urge to get into the Common Market at almost any cost. The result has been our undertaking burdens both in real terms and across the exchanges to get in which are going to make the very objects supposed to be gained by joining the Common Market considerably more difficult to achieve as we shall see later, at least unless the terms presently agreed are substantially renegotiated. The electorate generally has got more and more depressed and irritated by the miserable economic performance it has been witnessing, and it is surely no coincidence that the most violent swings in public opinion have occurred at times of deflation. The trade union movement, having obtained no advantage from policies of wage restraint during periods of deflation now regularly supports wage claims which bear no relation to any conceivable gains in productivity. But if there is no rational policy to follow which produces real wage increases, a policy of grab-what-you-can, particularly if this is what is going on in other sections of society all the time, is not an unnatural corollary. It is not a happy situation when it is more profitable to invest in property, old postage stamps, furniture and works of art than it is to invest in almost any form of productive industry, yet such is the situation in Britain now.

Is all this failure really inevitable? Is the present mood of fatalism and pessimism really warranted? Clearly, Britain has got the economic cards stacked against her to some extent, but is our economic predicament really such that it is impossible for better results to be achieved? The thesis of this book is not only that all these problems are soluble, but also that the solutions are perfectly practicable within our existing political and economic framework. The procedure adopted to tackle the problems falls into two halves. In Chapter II a comprehensive analysis is developed so that all our economic objectives can be ranked and weighted with their various points of interaction spelt out. Armed with the results of this analysis in Chapter III the economic problems facing Britain are tackled, and a plan developed which over a five year period should transform our economic circumstances. Since one of the results of the theoretical section in Chapter II is to enable us to make direct overall comparisons between the efficiency of running economies one way rather than another, we are able to make an attempt to quantify how much better our new policy would be than the present one. In Chapter IV some of the political and social implications of a rapid change in Britain's economic prospects are discussed to round the picture off.

Method of Exposition

Before starting on the main sections of this book there are various points on the method of exposition adopted which should be made clear. Unfortunately the subject with which we are dealing is complex and difficult, but every effort has been made to cope with all the problems which have to be tackled with the minimum of jargon and in the simplest way. The subject is also unavoidably quantitative, and a little mathematics is inevitable. However, the mathematics too has been kept as simple as possible, and it is hoped that anyone with a reasonable school mathematics training should be able to follow all of it through. For those whose mathematical learning experience was some distance in the past there are appendices to remind you how to prove various points which are taken for granted in the main text for the sake of brevity. It is also to be hoped that the non-mathematical will be able to follow the general line of argument even if the algebraic steps involved in deriving the conclusions from the premises are shrouded in some mystery.

Some further points should be noted about the exposition which follows. In the first place every effort has been made to try to deal with all the problems as they really are and to avoid the wishful thinking which has characterised so many efforts to cope with Britain's economic problems in the past, not least in the National Plan. By the same token at all stages, both in the theoretical and practical sections, the margins for error with which we are dealing are carefully assessed because any plan which depends for its execution either on nothing or on not very much going wrong is doomed to failure. A further point which has been borne very carefully in mind is the cost in time and energy involved in institutional changes, whether they involve reorganising Whitehall, imposing import tariffs, nationalising or denationalising industries, imposing restrictions on wage and price rises, etc., etc. Some or all of these policies may be necessary but there is a grave danger with any such changes that the effort involved in the mechanics of making the changes distracts attention from the real problems without providing any actual solutions.[6] Radical changes may be required but their cost in relation to their effectiveness must be carefully considered, and in the prescriptions which follow there will be found a strong bias in favour of changes which can be put into effect simply and quickly with the minimum of administrative upheaval.

Finally, it will be noted that the exposition which follows is in a low emotional key. It is a largely apolitical attempt to get to grips with the problems which face us, although Chapter IV is more concerned with political implications. It is really an attempt to see whether after all Britain's economic predicament is still amenable to a rational liberal democratic solution.

Chapter II Welfare Analysis

Part 1 Introduction

The aim of this chapter is to carry out a systematic investigation into the claims of different economic policy objectives for priority, and to develop a method of assessing the overall results which can be achieved from any mixture of policy decisions which it is possible to make. Once this has been done it is possible to work out optimum policy combinations allowing for the interaction between conflicting objectives. This approach to the problem in hand is referred to in the chapter which follows as Welfare Analysis. However, in this book we shall need a synonym for welfare to which we can apply a tight and rather technical definition, and for this purpose we shall use the word 'benefit'.

Definition of Benefit

To enable us to place our agreed economic objectives in order of importance, with quantitative weights attached, it is necessary to have one over-riding policy objective to which all others can be related. The usual economic objective of maximum output per unit of input, or some variation on this theme, will not do because we specifically want to move away from the basically static situations to which this type of analysis relates. The main reason why this is so is that static, or even comparatively static, analysis needs to use ordinary financial units to relate to the real world, and the first thing we want to do is to break away from this restraint. To deal with all our objectives it is impossible to value what the economy produces in money terms even at constant prices, particularly when trying to assess the value of growth as a policy goal. But we also want to investigate whether output in a year's time is worth as much as output now, whether £1,000 million added to the National Income when it is running at an annual rate of £20,000 million is worth the same as when it is running at an annual rate of £40,000 million, whether the same National Income is worth as much if it is gained with a high level of unemployment as with a low level, whether a high rate of inflation reduces its value in real terms and other matters where financial units are not appropriate.

What we shall do, in fact, is to avoid working initially in financial units at all but to construct a model based on an entity which we shall call economic benefit, or just benefit for short. We shall find that when the model is fully developed it is not at all difficult to relate the results back to financial units so that the step we are now taking is not one which takes us away from the real world. We shall define a unit of benefit as being the whole economic reward which would be received from the economy this year assuming that this year's total output had been achieved with no unemployment of labour or under-utilisation of existing capital resources or changes in the value of money or changes in the population or labour force, with international payments in perfect balance, with no net investment but no disinvestment, and with no changes in the distribution of wealth or income. Now if there was any unemployment, changes in the value of money, etc. this year then the benefit derived from the economy would alter. It should also be noticed that net investment will reduce current benefit but should increase it in the future. Next year, in fact, the economy will produce another different amount of benefit. It will also be a year's distance away in time, and may therefore be considered less valuable as seen from now. In the next and subsequent years again there will be different amounts of benefit produced. Taking into account all the factors which can affect benefit as thus defined we shall then take as our maximand the largest value we can obtain for all the benefit for this year and every year in the future added together, allowing for the fact that we may think that benefit in the future less worth having than benefit now.

Of the policy objectives which we are considering it will be noted that economic growth has a cumulative quality not possessed by the others. This should suggest that the gains in terms of benefit from economic growth could be of a rather special order of magnitude. The procedure we shall follow therefore is to hold all the other desiderata in limbo for the time being while we build up our model for benefit considering simply economic growth. In other words we shall assume initially that any level of economic growth can be achieved without any balance of payments difficulties, changes in the value of money, unemployment of labour or capital resources, or changes in the distribution of wealth or income. We shall also assume for the time being that there are no changes in the population as a whole, or the proportion of the population in employment. All these assumptions will be removed later one by one, and it will be seen then that the influence of each of our objectives on our maximand is unaffected by the order in which they are dealt with so that the procedure being followed is perfectly fair.

The starting point for producing an optimum economic policy for growth, our first task, is to take the economy at the size it is and to divide all the output there is into two categories, consumption and investment. Broadly speaking investment should be construed as any output which produces more output in future, and consumption, *per contra*, as any output which is consumed now and therefore has no effect on future output. In fact there are a considerable number of hard cases which will be treated in detail later; at this stage it is only necessary to establish the main principle. However, quite apart from the question of hard cases, there are various points about investment which must be made now to make the position clearer.

First there is a very important distinction to be made between the private and social rates of return to investment. If the average holder of a capital sum invests his money he will be very lucky if, net of inflation, he receives an income from his investment of much more than 10% p.a., and a figure of 5% p.a. would probably be much nearer the average, and this would be before tax. However, it does not follow from this that the gain to the economy as a whole from his investment was only 5-10%; typically it is very much higher, perhaps 20-40%, and often higher than that. Where does the different go? The answer is that some of it goes in wage and salary increases to those operating and managing the investment, a good deal of it goes in tax, and often some of the surplus is reinvested. This distinction between the private and social rates of return on investment is extremely important. From the point of view of the model we are developing it must be clearly undertsood that it is the social rate of return with which we are concerned.[1]

Secondly, it must be realised that investment as we are now using this term covers public and private investment, and that it includes investment in such things as roads which do not show an immediate financial return to anyone because they are not charged for, although they do show a return to the economy as a whole because more rapid transport cuts down costs generally.

Thirdly, it is in fact the case that the social rate of return on different investments varies very widely, a point we shall return to later. However, at this stage what we are concerned with is the average rate of social return on investment, taking into account all the investments made over any particular period of time.

Fourthly, not all investment is net investment. Within any accounting period a certain amount of existing producer goods are scrapped and have to be replaced, and indeed in Britain over the last twenty years nearly half of the gross investment made has been for replacement purposes. This is a factor which will cause us some problems, but at this stage let it be said that the model which we are building is based on the assumption that it is only net investment which produces additional output in future, and that replacement investment does nothing more than replace what was already there. At first sight this may not appear a very satisfactory way of dealing with this problem, because it is of course very likely that any new replacement investment will embody technical progress and therefore be more productive than what it replaced. However, this problem is not as serious as might appear at first sight, and at this stage we will just bear it in mind, and deal with it in more detail later on.

Having introduced the two categories of output to be considered, consumption and investment, and outlined the type of return on investment which we are concerned with, there is one very important point about consumption as against investment which must be made. We shall make the reasonable assumption that benefit is derived from consumption and not investment, or in other words that it is the consumption element in output which we want to maximise, and that investment is only desirable in so far as it increases consumption in the future and not for itself.

As regard consumption there are two other factors which must be given their due weight. One is that we may not think that consumption in the future is as valuable as consumption now, and the other is that we may not think that the increased benefit from the same absolute size of increase in the National Income would be the same at different levels, e.g. that an increase in National Income from £20,000 million to £21,000 million would not cause the same increase in benefit as one from £10,000 million to £11,000 million. The first of these two factors is usually called the rate of discount of the future, and the second the declining marginal utility of income. The idea of discounting the future is one which is fairly easy to grasp, and we shall find that it is not difficult to build up a model incorporating this concept without for the moment knowing what a reasonable rate for discounting the future would be. However, we cannot even begin without investigating the declining marginal utility of income and this subject must be tackled before we can get any further.

Part 2   The Growth Model

The Declining Marginal Utility of Income[2]

The first step to be taken is to make the assumption that we can treat the benefit derived from the whole economy as being the aggregate benefit of all the individual people who make up the economic community. The reason for taking this step is that it is much easier to get to grips with the concept of the declining marginal utility of income if it can be visualised in terms of individuals rather than the whole community. Let us in fact consider an average individual.

As a start it is worth asking whether the marginal utility of incomes falls at all? The answer to this question is not at all obvious over small increases, but common sense tells us that an extra £1 must make less difference to a person with an income of £100,000 than to one with an income of £1,000, and the implication must therefore be that the marginal utility of income must start falling somewhere. Taking the opposite view, does an increased income give any increased benefit at all? Paradoxically again the answer to this question is not absolutely obvious, and literature is full of comparisons between bliss in the cottage and anguish in the palace, or, more currently, the misery rather than happiness caused by winning the football pools. However, on closer investigation it is found that almost all these cases rely either on sudden access to wealth, or else refer to abnormal cases. As regards sudden access to great wealth, it has been well documented that this is a very disorientating experience[3] and that what in fact people want is a little more than they have at the moment rather than a huge amount more; rising benefit does imply time to adjust. As regards abnormal cases, a quotation from Sidgwick, one of the most careful investigators of the subject towards the turn of the last century, when it was more in vogue than it seems to be nowadays, would perhaps be in order:

> ". . . it remains true that the practical reasoning of the great mass of mankind — whether for themselves or for others in whom they are individually interested — proceeds on the assumption that it is an advantage to be richer; and further, that the judgment of the most highly cultivated, scrupulously moral and sincerely religious persons — as expressed in their conduct — does not diverge materially from that of the vulgar in the matter. The élite certainly disagree very much with the vulgar as to the real value of particular purchasable commodities; but they do not practically doubt that additional control over purchasable commodities generally is an important gain to an individual who obtains it. A man who chose poverty for himself, except for some manifest special and unpurchasable advantage, or at the manifest call of some special duty, would be deemed an eccentric; a man who chose it for his wife and children would be generally thought to deserve a harsher name."[4]

In sum, common sense and obversation (combined perhaps with Victorian social certainty) are the best guide, and, particularly if the acute disbenefit caused by a falling income is born in mind, we can safely say that at least at some point the marginal utility of income does fall, though a caution would have to be introduced that the whole concept should be operating above subsistence level as below it quite different factors would apply.

Is it feasible to take a less cautious view and try to establish how marginal utility of income falls by direct observation? Several proposals have been put forward as to ways of doing so and we must consider these in turn, because it would be a great help to our analysis if this important matter could be cleared up beyond doubt.

First it has been suggested that a schedule could be drawn up of the order in which the average man disposes of his income as it gets larger, and, on the assumption that he is out to maximise the benefit he gets from it, a direct comparison could be made between the benefit to be gained by an expenditure of £2,000 p.a. and £1,000 p.a. by comparing the number of the same goods bought at different income levels. However it does not take long to see that any such procedure is really begging the question; at best it is pushing the problem back to comparing, say, two motor cars one worth £2,000 p.a. as against one worth £1,000 p.a. But since motor cars and money are interchangeable we are no further forward.

A second way of tackling the problem which has been proposed is to get at the marginal utility of income by seeing how hard people are prepared to work for the last £1 which they earn. This approach suffers from formidable practical difficulties to do with marginal rates of taxation, but, even apart from this problem, empirical investigation of the hours which people work does not show any marked correlation between income and hours worked at all. Indeed some of the most highly paid people work the longest hours. Of course some of the explanation for this fact lies in the type of work being done; more highly paid work is generally more interesting and rewarding *per se*, but as soon as this kind of factor is introduced the validity of this approach to the problem is totally undermined. Nor are comparisons over time any help; indeed, if anything, the working week is actually rising at the moment, and a survey carried out in Britain in the mid sixties showed that 55% of the population would prefer to work even longer hours if they were paid for it.[5] Thus attempts to get at the marginal utility of income by considering demands for more income as against leisure throw no useful light at all on the problem in hand.

Much the same can be said about tackling the subject via the proportion of their incomes which people save. One difficulty here is that the amount which people do save alters erratically and it is well known that savings, far from being carefully planned, at least at the margin are often a residual left over after expenditure has been made, and therefore are unlikely to be a reliable guide. But a far more serious difficulty arises when one considers what people save for; the reason is nearly always so that either more money can be spent in the future, or else existing borrowings can be paid off. As both of these reasons imply shifting expenditure patterns forwards or backwards through time, rather than savings being something separate and different from expenditure, the case for using savings to measure the declining marginal utility of income also collapses completely.

Another proposal[6] is that it would be possible to measure the declining utility of income by a process of probability analysis. The idea here is that people should be offered let us say a £100 p.a. rise and then asked what probability of having a £200 p.a. rise instead they would accept. If such questions were asked of enough people at different levels of income a complete picture could be built up of the way the marginal utility of income falls. At first sight this appears to be a conceptually sounder scheme, but on closer investigation there are again major problems. First, there are some 15,000 betting shops in the U.K. all making a handsome living for their proprietors because people's desire for a flutter evidently far outweighs any effect which the declining marginal utility of income may have upon them. The empirical difficulties involved in isolating an investigation from anyone who was prepared to gamble with the odds against them — virtually all gamblers — would appear to exclude most of the population and thus leave a somewhat unrepresentative sample at the end. And even if this problem could be overcome one would still be left with the gap between what people say that they will do and what they will actually do when it comes to the point of decision, which would make the results achieved unreliable. It seems that probability analysis fares no better than the other proposals.

Does this inability to pin down the exact way in which marginal utility of income declines mean that nothing more can reasonably be said except that it must start declining somewhere? It might appear that we have reached a dead end, but this is not really the case. The problem with trying to measure the falling marginal utility of income directly is that we are trying to attain a greater degree of precision than is possible or than we really need. A much more fruitful procedure is to choose as simple an assumption as possible, which puts the minimum claim on one's credulity, but which must make it possible to compare the amount of benefit received from one income level as against another; it is also very important that the margins of possible or likely error involved in such an assumption should be testable. In other words, the best tactic is not to search for empirical evidence for the exact relationship between income and benefit, but to make common sense assumptions about what the relationship is likely to be and then show that even if this relationship was quite widely different the implications for our model would be quite small.

There is in fact a wide consensus of opinion as to at least the general relationship between income and benefit. Nearly all investigators have come to the broad conclusion that benefit increases as the logarithm of income, although some commentators[7] have been inclined to think that benefit increases less rapidly, while others have found that practical experience of the world suggests that if anything the reverse is the case. Nevertheless almost all are agreed that the general relationship between income and benefit must be of a logarithmic nature, i.e. that an increase in income of £100 p.a. for someone with an income of £1,000 p.a. gives about the same increase in benefit as an increase of £200 p.a. for someone with an income of £2,000 p.a. This is a relationship which is simple, which does accord with common sense, and which is also mirrored in the way people behave in the real world over such matters as maintaining income differentials and attitudes to progressive taxation. We shall therefore assume for the time being that this is an exact description of the relationship between benefit and income, although later we shall test carefully the strength of the assumption that the relationship is quite as exact as that. Finally we must notice again that the concepts discussed here relate to people above subsistence level; below this level it would be implausible to assume any such relationship as we have discussed here.

It will be recalled that this analysis of the relationship between income and benefit has been concerned entirely with the individual. We now want to generalise our conclusions and apply them to the whole economy, but before doing so we must tackle the argument that there are side effects from each individual's income going up which mean that in aggregate the increase in benefit is less than one would hope for by adding up each individual increase in benefit. This is the external diseconomy argument in another guise — one man's motor car is the next man's traffic jam. This is a fashionable argument nowadays, and no-one would deny the dangers of congestion, despoliation of the countryside, exhaustion of natural resources, pollution and all the other hazards to our ecology. However, it is important to keep a sense of proportion about these matters and indeed to keep them in historical perspective because there is nothing new about threats to our environment; they have been there throughout history. All that is necessary for our argument is to show that there is no good reason to believe that the ratio between increased output and increasing diseconomies is altering unfavourably. Probably the fairest assessment is that in some areas we are doing better than average and in others worse, but there seems to be no reason for believing that the overall ratio is deteriorating, especially in view of the very widespread concern about environmental matters. We shall therefore assume that we can generalise from the individual back to the whole economy while asking the sceptics to note that there is no reason why society should not make a political decision to spend more of its increased resources on environmental protection if their fears materialise. It may indeed be that this would be one of the most rewarding areas in which an increasing national income could be spent.

A rather different objection to generalising from the individual to society as a whole is that the arguments put forward to justify the logarithmic relationship between benefit and income are couched in terms of rather old fashioned private consumption and do not adequately recognise the extent to which benefit is a function of services and amenities provided on a communal basis by the state, and of leisure. None of these enter into the individual's income, at least post tax, if income is measured in purely financial terms. However, our general approach to the problem of measuring what the economy is providing for the people who compose it can rescue us easily from this charge. We are certainly considering income and the benefit which accrues from it in the widest sense to include all the good things in life which depend directly or indirectly on economic resources for their attainment, and this, of course, includes leisure as well as goods and services provided both publicly and privately.

Introduction of Notation

We are now in a position to start on the model building process proper and since the essence of this analysis is to get to grips with priorities in a quantitative rather than qualitative fashion, the concepts which have been introduced so far need to be put into a form in which they can be subjected to mathematical treatment. It is necessary, therefore, to introduce some notation for them. The notation will be kept as simple as possible but will be used again and again throughout the rest of this book, and should therefore be carefully absorbed. The notation to be used is as follows:

C — the proportion of the net output of the economy which is consumed: more precisely, the proportion of the net national product at factor cost which is consumed. The value of C would be 1.0 if all the output was consumed, and 0.0 if it was all invested.

I — the proportion of the net output of economy which is invested: again more strictly, the proportion of the net national product at factor cost which is invested. Here too the value of I would be 1.0

if all the output was invested, and 0.0 if all the output was consumed.

It will be noted as a matter of definition that $C + I = 1$.

R – the social rate of return on investment. For the moment we are assuming no changes in the size of the labour force, and that all investment has a one year gestation period; we are also assuming that R is constant over time. All these assumptions will be relaxed later. A value for R of, say, 0.25 thus means that a net investment of £1,000 million p.a. this year will produce extra output of £250 million next year.

D – the factor by which consumption in one year's time should be discounted as against consumption this year. Thus a value for D of 1.0 implies no discount at all, and one of 0.9 implies a rate of discount of 10% p.a. This factor obviously has some relation to the concept of interest rates though as we shall see it is not strictly comparable.

d – the factor which has already been discussed at some length to allow for the declining marginal utility of income.

B – the benefit which would have been obtained from the economy this year if this year's output had been achieved with no unemployment of labour or capital resources, or changes in the value of money, or changes in the population or labour force, with international payments in perfect balance, with no net investment but no disinvestment, and with no changes in the distribution of wealth or income.

B_0 – the benefit from consumption this year. The same provisos hold for B_0 as for B, except that we are now allowing for some net investment. As we have already posited that benefit arises from consumption only, and not investment, any rate of net investment implies that C is less than unity so that B_0 will be less than B. We will also assume that the ratio between B and B_0 is the same as between 1.0 and C. Since we are taking it that the marginal utility of income falls, it will always in fact be the case $B_0/B > C/1$, but as long as C is reasonably close to unity this assumption is not a very strong one and in any case any bias which is introduced by this assumption is systematic in that it affects every year equally, so that it will not affect at all the optimum ratios which we are looking for.

B_1 – the benefit from consumption next year, on the same basis as B_0 except that we will now have factors D and d in operation.

B_n — the benefit from consumption n years from now, on the same basis as B_1, i.e. with factors D and d in operation. This is the general term.

It will also help in the intermediate analysis to use the following notation:

b_0, b_1, b_2 etc — the benefit from consumption in this year, next year, the year after etc. without factors D and d in operation.

Finally we must have a notation for the maximand we are aiming for and this is as follows:

ΣB — the sum of all the benefit gain from this year and every other year in the future, allowing for factors D and d.

Σb — for intermediate analysis, the sum of all the benefit gained from this year and all the years in the future not allowing for factors D and d.

We shall refer to ΣB in the text as 'total benefit'.

Let us now start by noting the following identities which follow from the definitions set out above: First, as already mentioned, by definition $C + I = 1$; it therefore follows that $C = (1 - I)$ and $I = (1 - C)$. Secondly, we have already made the assumption that $B_0/B = C/1$ from which it follows that $CB = B_0$.

Now we have already defined B as being a unit of benefit and therefore B can be taken as being equal to 1; from this it follows that $C \times 1 = B_0$, i.e. that $C = B_0$.

Derivation of Optimum Savings/Investment Ratios

Let us now consider values for b_0, b_1 etc. We have already seen that $b_0 = C$, but since in this year we are in our base year, neither factors D nor d can be in operation, and it therefore follows that $B_0 = b_0$, the first value we are looking for. Next year, by the definitions above, the output of the economy will have increased as a result of this year's net investment, the measurement of which is I, and since for the time being we are ignoring factors D and d we can work in financial units, from which it follows that the extra output next year will be $I \times R$. However, not all the extra output will be consumed because some of it will need to be reinvested. How much? The answer is that since all the assumptions we have made are the same whatever the income level we started from, as long as it is not below subsistence, it follows that the optimum values of C and I must be the same every year, although at this stage we do not know what these values should be.

Thus the value of b_1 must be $C + IRC$

$$= C(1 + IR)$$

By a similar process of argument it can be deduced that the value of b_2 must be $b_1 + b_1 IR$

$$= b_1(1 + IR)$$

$$= C(1 + IR)^2$$

and from this it can easily be seen that the value of

$$b_n = C(1 + IR)^n$$

Incidentally, we may note at this stage that evidently each of the terms in the series for b_0, b_1, b_2 etc. is larger than the last, so that if we added together all the terms for this year and all future years their sum would be infinite.

Let us now consider what would happen to the values of b_0, b_1, b_2 etc. allowing for factor D, but assuming for the moment that factor d does not need to be allowed for. As previously, the first term for b_0 would be C, but next year's benefit as viewed from this year would have to be reduced by multiplying it by factor D, i.e. instead of being b_1 it would be $b_1 D$. We must now make the assumption that D remains constant from one year to the next. This does not sound an unreasonable assumption to make, but we shall see later that it makes very little difference if D does change over time. Assuming now that D does not alter, it follows that the value of b_2 will have to be reduced to $b_2 D^2$, and similarly n years from now the value of b_n will have to be reduced to $b_n D^n$. Substituting back into the first series produced we get the following new results for benefit in this and following years:

This year   — C

Next year   — $C(1 + IR)D$

Year after   — $C(1 + IR)^2 D^2$

In n years   — $C(1 + IR)^n D^n$

Again in passing, we may note that we can treat these yearly values as the terms of a series and the sum of this particular series is $C/1 - (1 + IR)D$ which may or may not have a meaningful value depending on whether $1 > (1 + IR)D$. The steps involved in producing this and subsequent summations have not been included in the text for the sake of brevity of exposition, but they will all be found laid out in Appendix A.

Let us now consider what happens to the values of b_0, b_1, b_2, etc. allowing for factor d operating, but this time, for the moment, ignoring factor D. Now we know from the series that we have evaluated already that $b_0 = C$, and $b_1 = C(1 + IR)$. However, whatever values of C, I, and R are chosen which fall within the bounds of reason, the difference between b_0 and b_1 cannot be very great, so let us make the assumption that *between these two years only* (this year and next year) the difference in benefit is so small that factor d can be ignored. We can then arrive at the difference in benefit between next year and this year by subtracting b_0 from b_1 — i.e.:

$$C(1 + IR) - C$$
$$= C + CIR - C$$
$$= CIR$$

Now from our investigation into the falling marginal utility of income, we have already come to the conclusion that the most reasonable way of allowing for factor d is to assume that equal proportional income increases give an equal increase in benefit, and we also posited that if this is true for the average individual it must be true for the population as a whole. Therefore if there is the same proportional rise in consumption every year — and we can easily see that this is so by inspecting the terms for b_0, b_1, b_2, etc. — it follows that the increase in benefit derived from the economy each year must be the same, *viz CIR*. Thus the values for b_0, b_1, b_2, etc. allowing for factor d but not D are as follows:

This year   — C

Next year   — $C + CIR$ or $C(1 + IR)$

Year after   — $C + 2CIR$ or $C(1 + 2IR)$

In n years   — $C + nCIR$ or $C(1 + nIR)$

As each term in this series is also larger than the one before it follows again that the series diverges, i.e. the sum increases indefinitely as the number of terms increases. The relationship between income and benefit is conceptually difficult and there are some problems involved in using a linear function to compare the difference in benefit between this year and next year, and a logarithmic function to compare benefit for all subsequent years. Those interested in more detailed justification of the arguments presented here are referred to Appendix B where possible lines of criticism are discussed.

Let us now return to our series and combine together the series allowing for factor D with the one allowing for factor d. This new series will give us yearly values of benefit allowing for both factors D and d together, which is the series for B_0, B_1, B_2, etc. whose sum ΣB is the maximand we are looking for. As previously the value for the first term B_0 is C. The value for the second term B_1 is the value obtained for b_1 allowing for d, which is $C(1 + IR) \times D$ – i.e. $B_1 = C(1 + IR)D$. Similarly the value for $B_2 = C(1 + 2IR)D^2$. Laying the values out as previously for the benefit obtained in this and subsequent years the terms are as follows:

$$\text{This year} \quad - \quad B_0 = C$$
$$\text{Next year} \quad - \quad B_1 = C(1 + IR)D$$
$$\text{Year after} \quad - \quad B_2 = C(1 + 2IR)D^2$$
$$\text{In } n \text{ years} \quad - \quad B_n = C(1 + nIR)D^n$$

To evaluate the sum of this series it is necessary to split it into two sets of terms by multiplying C and the terms in D into the brackets. The series then becomes:

$$B_0 = C$$
$$B_1 = CD + CIRD$$
$$B_2 = CD^2 + CIRD^2$$
$$\text{and } B_n = CD^n + nCIRD^n$$

Again without proof here, although it will be found in Appendix A, the sum of the first series of terms is $C/(1 - D)$ and of the second $CIRD/(1 - D)^2$, i.e.:

$$\Sigma B = \frac{C}{(1 - D)} + \frac{CIRD}{(1 - D)^2}$$

$$= \frac{C}{(1 - D)} \left\{ 1 + \frac{IRD}{(1 - D)} \right\}$$

$$= \frac{C}{(1 - D)^2} \left\{ (1 - D) + IRD \right\}$$

This expression can now be written in terms of either C or I only, since $C + I = 1$. Writing it in terms of I only it becomes:

$$\Sigma B = \frac{C}{(1-D)^2}\left[(1-D) + RD(1-C) \right]$$

$$= \frac{C}{(1-D)^2}(1-D+RD-RDC)$$

$$= \frac{C - CD + RDC - RDC^2}{(1-D)^2}$$

$$= \frac{1 - D + IRD - I + ID - I^2RD}{(1-D)^2}$$

$$= \frac{(1-D) + I(RD - 1 + D) - I^2RD}{(1-D)^2}$$

To find the maximum value of ΣB the procedure to be followed now is to differentiate the expression for ΣB given above with respect to I, first rearranging the terms slightly:

$$\text{If } \Sigma B = \frac{(1-D) + I(RD - 1 + D) - I^2RD}{(1-D)^2}$$

$$= \frac{(1-D)}{(1-D)^2} + I\frac{(RD - 1 + D)}{(1-D)^2} - I^2\frac{RD}{(1-D)^2}$$

$$\text{then} \quad \frac{d\Sigma B}{dI} = \frac{RD - 1 + D}{(1-D)^2} - 2I\frac{RD}{(1-D)^2}$$

Now the maximum possible value of ΣB is obtained when the value of $\frac{d\Sigma B}{dI}$ is set at zero,

$$\text{i.e. when } \frac{RD - 1 + D}{(1-D)^2} = 2I\frac{RD}{(1-D)^2}$$

$$\text{i.e. when } I = \frac{RD - 1 + D}{2RD}$$

This is the optimum saving/investment ratio we are looking for.

It will be noted that the procedure adopted here implies that values for I and R are independent of each other. This is a very important assumption and we shall have to consider later the extent to which I

and R can be regarded as truly independent, and whether, if they are not independent their relationship is inverse, as is often assumed, or the reverse. At this stage we will assume that there is no necessary relationship between I and R and leave our options open until the evidence is considered.[8]

Let us now review the situation to date. What has been achieved so far is a quantitative measure of the benefit now and in the future which is being produced from the economy — ΣB or total benefit — in terms of the potential output which is achievable this year. This is an important point because it means that the values for total benefit are independent of the value of national income per head (provided the economy is above subsistence level) and also they are independent of the size of the economy. We have also derived an expression which we shall call I_{opt} which is the optimum amount of the net national product which should be saved and invested as against being consumed. However, this point has been reached without much having been said about either D or R, without a clear definition of I and C and without dealing with a fair number of other assumptions, several of which involve important policy objectives in their own right. There are also several assumptions which have been made during the process of deriving mathematical expressions for the maximands which we are interested in, and it is very important that the margins of error involved in these assumptions should be checked carefully to ensure that the conclusions reached are soundly based. Finally, nothing has yet been said about how to move to any optimum policy mix from the present one either in theory or in practice. The rest of this chapter will be devoted to all these topics in turn except for the very last, putting the policy into practice, which will take up the whole of the next chapter using the United Kingdom economy as it is to show how the results of the theoretical exercise in this chapter can be put into effect.

Discounting the Future

Let us now see what can be said about an appropriate value, or appropriate values, for D, and let us ask first of all whether there is a case for discounting the future at all. It must be said straight away that many eminent writers on this subject have thought not. Ramsey, whose article 'A mathematical theory of savings' published in the *Economic Journal* in 1928 first aroused interest in optimal savings and investment ratios, was against discounting the future, and so was Pigou who followed up Ramsey's ideas after the latter's early and untimely death. Their main reasons for taking this attitude was that they thought it unethical to treat future generations as being less important than our own. However, the 'no discount' approach has a number of grave objections to it. On a purely theoretical plane, even if we were for the moment to accept the Ramsey/Pigou ethical argument, is it not rational to assume that there is at least some chance that the world as we know it will come to an end via a nuclear holocaust? Even a small probability of this happening implies a value for D of something less than unity. Apart from this point there is a further difficulty with this ethical argument arising from the asymmetry between our generation and those in the future. If any growth of national product per head at all is achieved, future generations are going to enjoy a higher standard of living than we do brought about at least in part by our efforts for which they will effectively pay nothing. Are we really under a still greater obligation to do more than this, to sacrifice even more today so that in the indefinite future our descendents enjoy undreamed of wealth? And will this point ever arrive, because should every generation scrimp and save for those to follow and never enjoy a substantial proportion of the fruits of previous investment which might be available to it? This does not sound a very practical policy prescription. In any case the whole 'future generations' argument is unrealistic because there is no clear dividing line between this generation and the next; generations overlap all the time. The intermingling of generations which results makes possible a reasonable balance being struck between the old and the young, which is not so if generations are considered in isolation from each other.

From a more practical standpoint there are several other serious difficulties about the 'no discount' approach all of which relate to the fact that it does not square up to the observable facts of life. Why do people pay, and expect to receive interest if not because they discount the future? The unhappy history of the usury laws should demonstrate the unrealism of a 'no discount' policy. It also implies extremely high rates of reinvestment even if the return from investment is very low. Inspection of the expression for I_{opt} derived above shows that 50% of the net national product should be reinvested, if $D = 1$, irrespective of the value for R. It is difficult to believe that people would accept a state of affairs such as that as being reasonable and sensible. The conclusion to which we are therefore driven is that a 'no discount' approach has got no substantial theoretical or ethical backing and is also unrealistic and undemocratic. We shall therefore abandon 'no discount' and turn our attention to seeing what values of D involving some discount would be appropriate.

In trying to get at a quantitative value for D it might be thought that we had a rather better start than we did with d because there is some fairly obvious real world evidence to go on. Interest rates must bear some relation to the way people discount the future. However, the relationship is unfortunately very far from clear cut. First, there are some obvious difficulties to be overcome. Inflation affects the real rate of interest that people pay and receive, and allowance must be made not only for this factor but also for people's expectations about what they thought the rate of inflation was going to be, if they thought about it at all, as well as what the rate of inflation actually turned out to be. There are also problems to do with the risk of default, and with the fact that the rate of interest paid to lenders is often lower than that charged to borrowers because of administrative and advertising costs. However, it is not too difficult to get round these problems by considering rates of interest where none of these factors apply to any substantial extent. The yield on Consols would seem to be the most appropriate rate to consider and inspection of the records shows a fairly consistent picture. For example during the whole of the period from 1865 until the outbreak of the First World War the Consol rate never rose above 3.5% p.a. and never fell below 2.5% p.a. taking average figures for each year. However, the consistency of these results looks considerably less impressive when changes in the value of money are allowed for. Prices fell by an average of about 1¼% p.a. during the period from 1865 until the late 80's then remained more or less steady until the turn of the century, and then rose by nearly 2% p.a. on average until the outbreak of the First World War. None of these changes were reflected at all in the Consol rate. Since the First World War the results have been even more inconsistent, so that even if the Consol rate were a direct measure of factor D, we would not have a consistent value to choose.

In any case there are other difficulties about the Consol rate, even supposing it were consistent after allowing for the affects of changes in the value of money. One of the troubles about relating interest rates to the rates at which people discount the future is that there appears to be a lack of symmetry between borrowers and lenders which is likely to give a bias to whatever results emerge. Almost nobody wants to borrow money and pay interest on it unless it is required for spending on something, whether for purposes of investment or consumption. However, large numbers of people are quite happy to save and pile up cash balances even if they are earning no rate of interest on their savings at all. In this context it is a remarkable fact to note that the clearing banks in the U.K. have a total of over £5000m in current accounts on which virtually no interest is payable at all (only in the form of a small reduction in bank charges) and more than a further £4000m[9] in deposit accounts on which a low rate of interest is payable, and this at a time when the rate of inflation has been running a little short of 10% p.a.! This situation strongly suggests that the prime rate of interest, net of risk and all the effects of inflation, would still not be a satisfactory guide because if a considerable volume of savings is autonomous, and almost all borrowing is purposeful, then if the prime rate of interest is supposed to balance one against the other it will understate the rate at which people discount the future.

However, this is not the end of the problems with the prime rate of interest. Even supposing one could find a reliable average value and could overcome the problem of the bias described above one would still be left with the uneasy feeling that the whole business of prime rates of interest is too much the subject of administrative control to be a very reliable guide. Furthermore, it is perfectly clear from the interest rates which people are prepared to pay, even net of inflation (for hire purchase transactions for example), that many people do appear to discount the future by a very much larger amount than one would gather by simply looking at the rate on Consols, and we have seen already the rates of interest which people are prepared to pay when they are borrowing may well be more significant than the rate at which people are prepared to lend. The very fact there is a difference is what keeps banks and finance going. Let us therefore turn our attention to the rates at which finance companies lend to see whether they throw any more definite light on appropriate values for D.

Unfortunately this line of investigation is open to serious objections too. In the first place many people are so confused by the effects of inflation and the misleading way in which many hire purchase forms are drawn up that they never have any clear idea what real rate of interest they are paying. In some cases the picture is made even more confusing by tax allowances which may mean that the real rate of interest being paid on money which is being borrowed is quite different from what is on the form. And what can we say about someone who, for example, pays a high rate of interest to buy a car on hire purchase knowing that his saving on rail fares will offset not only the interest he is paying but also the capital cost of the car and its running costs as well? Furthermore, if people borrow now intending to pay the money back later out of higher earnings — and there is a good deal of evidence that it is just these sort of people who do borrow a lot on hire purchase[10] — then factor *d* is back in the picture to make the confusion worse confounded.

Consideration of the activities of finance companies also leads on to another point of importance, relating to those who may well want to borrow but to whom finance companies will not lend because of their potential customers' lack of creditworthiness, even though they might well be prepared to borrow at very high interest rates indeed. This suggests that there are some people at least who discount the future at a very high rate, and indeed it should occasion no surprise to discover that there is a wide spread of rates at which people discount the future, perhaps correlated with age, social and educational backgrounds, intelligence and a host of other factors, What are we concerned with? Is it the average rate at which people *do* discount the future? Or at some point does the community give a right to restrain some peoples' very marked preference for the present as against the future biasing the average downwards? Are we perhaps concerned with the rate at which people *should* discount the future as against the rate at which empirical evidence suggests that they do?

These are difficult questions, and again, as with factor *d*, the only firm conclusion one can arrive at from all this confusing and conflicting evidence is that it would be quite impossible and unrealistic to give a precise quantitative measure of the value of *D*. However, again as in the case of *d*, it does not follow from this that nothing can be said at all. What the evidence we have considered suggests is that a rate of discount below 5% p.a. — giving *D* a value of .95 — would be unrealistic and undemocratic. It also suggests that one above 10% would bring us into an area where not many people would want to be net of all offsetting factors, and where in any case we may well be inclined to set restraints on the free play of democracy. This would give *D* a practical bottom limit of .9. Where within this band the 'right' value of *D* lies is up to each individual to decide. Perhaps surprisingly the actual value selected for *D* within this band is not very critical at all in terms of the policy recommendations which will emerge from the model we are constructing, but values outside this band do lead to considerably different conclusions as we shall see later.

Definition of Investment and Consumption

We must now turn to factors R and I, respectively the social rate of return on investment, and the proportion of the net output of the economy devoted to investment. Whereas with d and D it is fairly easy to understand intuitively what these factors are concerned with and the difficulties lie in quantifying their effects from very intangible evidence, with R and I there is any amount of statistical information available which is relevant to their values; the problems are those of definition and interpretation. Let us start with I.

Earlier on it was stated that broadly speaking investment would be defined as any expenditure which led to more output in the future and consumption, *per contra*, as any output which was consumed and therefore did not contribute to future output. It is easy to see from this definition that investment should include all expenditure on physical assets such as industrial plant and equipment, both in the public and private sectors, and should also comprise a good deal of social expenditure, e.g. on roads which improve communications and thus increase future output at least in the sense of reducing future inputs in relation to output. Starting at the other end of the scale it is not difficult to pick out a large range of expenditures which are clearly consumption such as food and drink, clothes, holidays, etc. There are also various types of government expenditure which evidently do not lead to future output of which one of the largest is on the armed services and which therefore should be treated as consumption. However, in the middle there are several hard cases, and although some of them are of such small magnitude that they can be safely ignored, there are several others which are of a very substantial size and which therefore deserve special comment. These are expenditures on housing, consumer durables, certain social services such as health in particular, and education. We must consider each of these in turn.

Expenditure on residential construction is treated in the National Income and Expenditure Blue Book as investment and it also produces a return in the form of rent in the rented sector, and the National Income is grossed up to allow for the benefits of owner occupation. It would appear, therefore, at first sight to qualify as investment for our purposes. This is especially so if another factor is taken into account, namely the fact that shortage of housing in the U.K. is often cited as being one of the causes of slow growth because it discourages labour mobility. Therefore in so far as expenditure on residential construction increases labour mobility, it would appear to contribute both directly and indirectly to future output. However, when one comes to quantify these benefits it turns out that the social rate of return on housing is extremely low, because, although housing construction is an extremely important social goal, the extra output which arises from residential construction is very little more than the rent, or imputed rent, which is generated. Perhaps this point can be made most clearly by asking: does investment in housing put up productivity in a cumulative fashion, which is really what I and R are concerned with? The answer is that it really does so only by a very small amount, and it therefore follows from this that we shall have to exclude residential construction from I, however much we may think that it should be treated as a top social priority for C.

Expenditure on consumer durables for personal use — cars, refrigerators, etc. — is not treated in the National Income and Expenditure Blue Book as investment, but nevertheless consumer durables are saved for and seen as investment by many people. Furthermore, in some respects they seem to qualify for inclusion in I in ways which housing does not seem to in that at least some consumer durables do put up peoples' productivity enormously. One only has to think of the effects of cars, washing up machines and vacuum cleaners. In addition, as the very name of consumer durables implies, the productivity gains resulting from them are not short-lived but last for some time. However, consumer durables suffer from one major disqualification from being included in I, and this derives from the fact that, although they push up productivity now, they do not lead to any additional cumulative output in future. This point can be brought out by considering the difference between a typewriter bought for use at home, which is in its way very productive, and a typewriter bought for use in an office, which becomes part of a productive process. The first is treated in the National Income and Expenditure Blue Book as personal consumption, and the second as investment in office equipment. This split does coincide with the dividing line which we would want to observe between I and C so that in this case we can feel contented with the normal national accounting conventions.

A considerable amount of expenditure in the government sector other than residential construction is treated in the national accounts as investment, although we may feel that it should not be included in I. Cases in point are expenditure on new hospitals, parks and sports grounds, and military installations. The question we must ask is always the same — do these expenditures lead to a cumulative increase in productivity in the future? Clearly the answer in nearly all such cases is that the productivity gains overall are likely to be too low for such expenditure to qualify as I rather than C. Are there other forms of government — or private — expenditure which are normally treated as consumption, but have the qualities of investment, so that we might like to include them not under C but under I? Apart from expenditure on education, which is a special case to be dealt with shortly, the answer must be no, even though a good deal of current expenditure, at least in the Health Service for example, does have some effect in increasing future output. The decisive factor, however, is that the average cumulative productivity gain from this type of expenditure is simply not high enough for any of this expenditure in total to be switched from one category to another.

This leaves us with the very large, and difficult case of education. Expenditure on education, except for capital expenditure on school buildings etc., is treated in the National Income and Expenditure Blue Book as being consumption and not investment. The cost of education is extremely heavy, especially if it is taken in the widest sense to include all forms of training. About a third of all those with a higher education are currently involved one way and another with teaching in Britain at the moment, and about 8% of the national income is spent on education. However, not only are these very heavy demands made on the limited national resources to provide teachers, buildings and equipment, but also there is a further heavy cost involved — this being the output foregone as a result of those receiving education spending a considerable amount of time doing so which would otherwise be spent in productive employment. However, although this expenditure is treated in the national accounts as being almost entirely current consumption, education if regarded as 'investment in man' does in fact fulfil all the criteria which we have laid down for inclusion under I rather C. In particular education has just that cumulative quality which we have looked for in vain with housing, consumer durables and various other types of government expenditure in that it leads to cumulatively more output in the future. The problem, though, with treating education simply as investment is that it also has many of the qualities of consumption. There is ample evidence that higher educational attainments not only lead to higher incomes, a reflection of higher productivity, but that they also lead to more enjoyment of life generally both at work and during leisure hours.[11] Indeed it seems that expenditure on education has a very special priority in that it can be regarded as both investment and consumption at the same time, a shared quality which cannot be attributed to any other form of expenditure at least to anything like the same extent. Perhaps this is just as well because although 'investment in man' is a very important type of investment both as regards what it costs and what it leads to, the actual social rate of return on investment is not very high − of the order of 15%[12] − so that it would be difficult to justify the very large current outlays on education purely on economic grounds without the concurrent social benefits.

It is worth noting at this point that the division employed in our model between consumption and investment is not quite the same as is commonly used, and it is this difference which has made it necessary to shift items of expenditure from one category to the other compared with conventional national income accounts. The distinction we are using is between what produces enjoyment or benefit − C − and what produces more output in the future − I. This should be compared with the conventional distinction between consumption and investment where investment is treated as being anything tangible produced during an accounting period which will produce some additional output in future, however little, and a residual which is consumption.[13]

The fact that the standard ways of producing national accounts do not square up with the division that our model requires between investment and consumption leaves us with two procedures available. We can either rewrite every set of national accounts which we have to deal with so that they do comply directly with our requirements; or we can see whether the net effects of the various changes between investment and consumption we should like to make would cancel out sufficiently closely for the broad national income ratios between I and C to be an adequately close approximation to what we might regard as the true I and C for any residual error to be unimportant. The first procedure of rewriting every set of accounts would be very tedious, so let us try the second.

Turning the National Income Blue Book, the following tables show the figures involved for the last two years for which they are available.

Capital expenditure treated as investment in the National Income Blue Book which we wish to treat as consumption because it will not lead to cumulatively more output in the future:

		All £m	
		1969	*1970*
National Health and Welfare ⎱	Central	128	139
Capital Expenditure ⎰	Local	37	41
50% Environmental Capital Expenditure		187	212
Military Capital Expenditure		20	25
Residential Construction	Public	817	769
	Private	686	696
Other Minor Items		14	13
		1,889	1,895

Expenditure treated as current in the National Income Blue Book which we wish to treat as 'Investment in Man':

	1969	*1970*
Current Public Expenditure on Education	1,579	1,758
Current Private Expenditure on Education	250[14]	275[14]
Educational Grants to Personal Sector	393	437
	2,222	2,470

The net result of all these changes is laid out below:

	1969	*1970*
Gross Domestic Capital Formation, including value of physical increase in stocks & WIP	8,495	9,340
Less: Capital Consumption	3,723	4,123
Net Domestic Capital Formation	4,772	5,217
Less: Investment Disallowed	(1,889)	(1,895)
Add: Investment in Man	2,222	2,470
New Total Net Domestic Investment	5,105	5,792

However, as we are treating education as being both consumption and 'Investment in Man' at the same time we have got to gross up the Net National Product to allow for the fact that we are getting a double benefit from expenditure on education, so we thus produce a further table showing the revised values for the Net National Product as follows:

	1969	1970
Net National Product per N.I. Blue Book	35,354	38,687
Add: Allowance for Double Benefit from Expenditure on Education	2,222	2,470
	37,576	41,157

Finally, we must now compare the ratios between our new figures for Net Investment and the Net National Product with the ratios derived from the National Income Blue Book using the conventional statistical practices. The results are as follows:

	1969	1970
Net investment as a proportion of net national product using:		
Standard accounting conventions	.1350	.1349
Our special accounting conventions	.1359	.1407

As can be seen, the difference between these ratios is so small that it can be safely ignored. Although we may not really like the way national income statistics are made up, for our purposes the conventional ways of treating consumption and investment will prove perfectly adequate, since within very narrow limits the effects of the changes we might like to make cancel out so that the ratios for I and C at the end of the day are barely altered from those obtained from conventional national accounts. It is a great help that this is so as the workability of our model would be considerably impaired if it were not possible to derive any practical results from it without reworking substantially all the data currently available. In fact we can use the broad statistical breakdowns exactly as they are in the normal published accounts without any reworking at all.

Before leaving the question of the dividing line between C and I some comment must be made about the measure of the size of the economy's output which is to be used when striking a ratio for net investment. There are two main ways in which the output can be measured — at market prices or factor cost — and at all times the figures presented in this book are at factor cost, because the taxes net of subsidies which inflate market prices only really affect consumption and do not, by and large, affect the prices of investment goods. Thus comparisons between market prices for consumption with what were in effect factor cost prices for investment (since market prices for investment goods are hardly inflated by taxes at all and thus are more or less equal to factor costs) would lend an undesirable bias. Incidentally, international comparisons are also more accurate on a factor cost than market price basis because of the fairly wide divergence between different tax systems in different countries. This still leaves the question of which measure of the economy's output we chose to adopt, and it may help those not too familiar with national income statistics to have the following table to peruse:

> Net Domestic Product
> Add: Net Property Income from Abroad
>
> Net National Product or National Income
> Add: Capital Consumption
>
> Gross National Product

Since it is taken for granted that the present capital stock must be made good every year — i.e. allowance must be made for depreciation — before a realistic measure of the national income can be struck, and since net property income from abroad is evidently income available for investment, the measure of the output of the economy used throughout this book for the ratios involving I and C is the net national product at factor cost. However, just to add to the confusion, it must be remarked that factor R, which is solely concerned with the results of domestic capital formation, can only be measured by increases in the net domestic product, since changes in property income from abroad are evidently not affected by domestic investment. The national income statistician's life would certainly be much simpler if the United Kingdom had a closed economy with no transactions involving other countries, and with no taxes!

Definition of the Social Rate of Return

Having now dealt with the problems of definition involving C and I we must now turn to R and get a clear picture of what this factor is measuring. Perhaps before doing so it should be stressed again that R is concerned with the *social* rate of return on investment and not the *private* rate, i.e. it is concerned with the total benefit received through the whole economy from an extra unit of investment — in increased wages, salaries, taxes and retained profit — as well as the return payable to whoever put the money up for the investment. In principle, measurement of R might not be thought to be all that difficult; all that should be involved would be to inspect the national accounts and see what net investment one year leads to by way of increased output in the next year. This is basically the ratio we are looking for. However, the situation is not as simple as that, and there are a number of complicating factors which we must tackle before a closely defined meaningful value for R can emerge and we must deal with these in turn. In particular, we must watch out closely for all those factors which determine why R should be found to have one value rather than another, because the model we are developing will be far more useful if it can explain such variations and predict fairly accurately what values of R will be obtained in the future, than if this cannot be done.

There are three types of factors which affect what we might call the 'crude' value of R obtained by simply inspecting the national accounts to see what increase in output this year resulted from last year's net investment. First, there is the fact that not all investment is net investment; second, other factor inputs can vary between one year and another, particularly employment; and third, even after allowing for these two influences there are still wide variations in the value of R obtained between different countries, and at different times in the same country. This is a very important area of our investigations and it is, of course, extremely important that we should be able to explain at least the principle causes of such variation. We shall also concentrate on seeing if there are good reasons for believing that values of I and R are likely to be correlated together either positively or negatively. In this chapter we shall consider some of the theoretical reasons for believing that the correlation is likely to be positive, given the right demand conditions, and in the next chapter we shall consider the empirical evidence.

Let us first of all consider the effects of the fact that not all investment is net investment — some of it is replacing existing worn out assets. However, the new investment is very likely to embody technical progress, so that at currently ruling prices it will have a lower capital/output ratio than whatever it replaces; certainly *on average* this is bound to be so as long as any technical progress is taking place. It follows from this that there will be an increase in output from the economy even if there is no net investment at all, and therefore if it is only net investment that is supposed to lead to extra output in our model, with replacement investment not yielding any increase, then the effectiveness of the net investment will be consistently overstated.

There is, of course, inevitably some substance in this charge but there are very good reasons for believing that the bias involved is not at all large, if it exists at all. In the first place, in times of steady inflation it is well known that the figure down in the accounts as 'capital consumption', which we have treated as the best available approximation to replacement investment, is consistently understated because the make up for this figure tends to depend on historic and not replacement costs. It follows from this, therefore, that the capital/output ratio of what is being scrapped is consistently understated probably to a point where the capital/output ratio of what is being disposed of is not all that far distant from what is replacing it. In any case, this must be a factor which reduces the bias we are concerned with to a considerable extent. Secondly, inspection of the type of investment carried out with different values of factor I lends credence to the supposition that net investment is a much better guide than gross investment to output increases. This is so because if I falls to a low level then it tends to have a much higher content of social investment in roads and residential construction, for example, and this has a low rate of economic social return compared to investment in manufacturing industry which typically rises much more rapidly than social investment when I increases.[15] The result is that even if R is overstated for very low values of I because of the effect of replacement investment, this effect is soon swamped once I reaches any size above, say, 0.1. Thirdly, inspection of national accounts for different countries and for the same country at different periods simply does not bear out the contention that R falls because of the gross/net investment problem; if anything it tends to rise. We will therefore ignore the gross/net investment problem on the sound grounds that its effect on the consistency of R, measured in terms of net investment, is minimal, and certainly swamped by much more potent influences from other directions.

The second major influence on R which we must consider is the other changes in factor inputs apart from changes in capital. In principle there are two other factor inputs which we ought to consider

— imports and labour. As regards imports, or more specifically import prices, there is nothing very much to be said, because if all our comparisons are made at constant prices (which necessarily they have to be) then changes in import prices affect the extent to which final output is deflated in a way which means that the effect on our measurement of R is automatically compensated for.

Changes in the size of the labour force, on the other hand, have a substantial and relatively easily measured effect on R. The simplest assumption to make is that broadly speaking every £100 increase in output involves a split in factor inputs which mirrors that for the economy as a whole. This implies some rather heroic adherence to the theory of marginal product if it is taken too literally, and partly for this reason, and partly for simplicity of calculation and comprehension, a somewhat arbitrary figure of exactly 75% has been used throughout the analysis that follows, although the error involved in sticking to this one figure is not believed to be very large. Thus the assumption made is that a 1% increase in employment leads to a ¾% increase in output provided that the capital stock remains the same. It should be noticed that the 1% relates to increases in those in employment, and not to any increases in those who may wish to work, an important point which we shall return to later.

Finally, we must deal with the other factors which effect the size of R. These again can be divided into two categories. On the one hand are what one might describe as micro economic factors, and on the other macro economic factors. The micro economic factors involve all kinds of ways of increasing the efficiency with which the economy can be run, from having fewer monopoly situations to better allocation of investment, from more education to higher mobility of labour. There is certainly a great deal that could be done to increase R via this type of policy prescription, and later on we shall put forward various new proposals for doing so, but by and large the scope which central government policy has for increasing R by fiat is limited, especially in the short term. Where the government undoubtedly can take steps to increase R — and this is by far the most important single influence on R as we shall see when we start looking at the relevant statistics — is to ensure that there is a high, and continuously high, pressure of demand so that all the investment which has been made is continuously kept in use. This is a point which we shall return to again and again when we turn to practical policy prescriptions.

Values for Total Benefit and Optimum Savings/Investment Ratios — in terms of Growth only

Having got to this point let us now look at the values for total benefit and I_{opt} which are thrown up by the formulae derived earlier and see what they show, taking values for D from .90 to .95, values for R from .05 to .40, and values for I in the expressions for total benefit from .05 to .40. Again at this stage we are assuming that there is no *necessary* relationship between I and R, and in particular we are assuming that I and R are not necessarily inversely related. These values are shown in the accompanying tables.

With regard to Table II.1 covering the optimum proportion of the

---

Table II.1

Table for I_{opt} for values of D from .90 to .95 plus unweighted average, and for values of R from .025 to .400.

$D \rightarrow$ R $\downarrow$	.90	.91	.92	.93	.94	.95	Unweighted Average
.025	(1.72)	(1.48)	(1.24)	(1.01)	(.78)	(.55)	(1.13)
.050	(.61)	(.49)	(.37)	(.25)	(.14)	(.03)	(.31)
.075	(.24)	(.16)	(.08)	.0	.074	.149	(.04)
.100	(.06)	.005	.065	.124	.181	.237	.093
.125	.056	.104	.152	.199	.245	.289	.174
.150	.130	.170	.210	.249	.287	.325	.229
.175	.183	.217	.252	.285	.318	.350	.267
.200	.222	.253	.283	.312	.340	.368	.296
.225	.253	.280	.307	.333	.358	.383	.319
.250	.278	.302	.326	.349	.372	.395	.337
.275	.298	.320	.342	.363	.384	.404	.352
.300	.315	.335	.355	.375	.394	.412	.364
.325	.329	.348	.366	.384	.402	.419	.375
.350	.341	.359	.376	.392	.409	.425	.384
.375	.351	.368	.384	.400	.415	.430	.391
.400	.361	.376	.391	.406	.420	.434	.398

Basis for Calculating Table:—

$$I_{opt} = \frac{RD - 1 + D}{2RD}$$

National Income to reinvest, the two main points which stand out are first the very high values of I_{opt} recommended, and secondly the consistency of this recommendation even with fairly high rates of discount of the future (i.e. low values for D) unless R also falls to very low levels. However Tables II.2 and II.3 for total benefit are more valuable, because, whereas Table II.2 only shows optimum values, the tables for total benefit show how closely suboptimal positions approach the optimum and are therefore much more useful in practical terms.

Table II.2

Values for ΣB for ranges of I from .05 → .40
R from .05 → .40
D from .90 → .95 + unweighted average

$D →$	.90	.91	.92	.93	.94	.95	Unweighted Average
R ↓	$I = 0.05$						
.05	9.71	10.82	12.22	14.02	16.45	19.90	13.86
.10	9.93	11.09	12.56	14.47	17.07	20.81	14.32
.15	10.14	11.36	12.90	14.92	17.69	21.71	14.79
.20	10.36	11.62	13.24	15.37	18.31	22.61	15.25
.25	10.57	11.90	13.58	15.83	18.93	23.51	15.72
.30	10.78	12.16	13.92	16.28	19.55	24.42	16.18
.35	11.00	12.42	14.26	16.73	20.17	25.32	16.65
.40	11.21	12.69	14.61	17.18	20.79	26.22	17.12
R ↓	$I = 0.10$						
.05	9.41	10.51	11.90	13.71	16.18	19.71	13.57
.10	9.81	11.01	12.54	14.57	17.35	21.42	14.45
.15	10.22	11.52	13.19	15.42	18.53	23.13	15.33
.20	10.62	12.02	13.84	16.27	19.70	24.84	16.22
.25	11.03	12.53	14.48	17.13	20.88	26.55	17.10
.30	11.43	13.03	15.13	17.98	22.05	28.26	17.98
.35	11.84	13.54	15.78	18.84	23.23	29.97	18.86
.40	12.24	14.04	16.43	19.69	24.40	31.68	19.75

Basis for calculating values for this table

$$\Sigma B = \frac{(1 - D) + I(RD - 1 + D) - I^2 RD}{(1 - D)^2}$$

Table II.2 (continued)

$D \rightarrow$	.90	.91	.92	.93	.94	.95	Unweighted Average
R ↓	$I = 0.15$						
.05	9.07	10.16	11.54	13.35	15.83	19.42	13.23
.10	9.65	10.88	12.46	14.56	17.50	21.85	14.48
.15	10.22	11.59	13.37	15.77	19.16	24.27	15.73
.20	10.80	12.31	14.29	16.98	20.83	26.69	16.98
.25	11.37	13.03	15.21	18.19	22.49	29.11	18.23
.30	11.94	13.74	16.12	19.40	24.15	31.54	19.48
.35	12.52	14.46	17.04	20.61	25.82	33.96	20.73
.40	13.09	15.17	17.96	21.82	27.48	36.38	21.98
R ↓	$I = 0.20$						
.05	8.72	9.79	11.15	12.95	15.42	19.04	12.84
.10	9.44	10.69	12.30	14.47	17.51	22.08	14.41
.15	10.16	11.59	13.45	15.98	19.60	25.12	15.98
.20	10.88	12.48	14.60	17.50	21.69	28.16	17.55
.25	11.60	13.38	15.75	19.02	23.78	31.20	19.12
.30	12.32	14.28	16.90	20.54	25.87	34.24	20.69
.35	13.04	15.18	18.05	22.06	27.96	37.28	22.26
.40	13.76	16.08	19.20	23.58	30.04	40.32	23.83
R ↓	$I = 0.25$						
.05	8.34	9.39	10.72	12.49	14.95	18.56	12.41
.10	9.19	10.44	12.07	14.27	17.40	22.13	14.25
.15	10.03	11.49	13.42	16.05	19.84	25.69	16.09
.20	10.88	12.55	14.77	17.83	22.29	29.25	17.93
.25	11.72	13.60	16.11	19.61	24.74	32.81	19.77
.30	12.56	14.65	17.46	21.39	27.19	36.38	21.60
.35	13.41	15.71	18.81	23.17	29.64	39.94	23.44
.40	14.25	16.76	20.16	24.95	32.08	43.50	25.28
R ↓		$I = 0.30$					
.05	7.95	8.96	10.26	11.99	14.41	17.99	11.93
.10	8.89	10.14	11.77	13.99	17.15	21.98	13.99
.15	9.84	11.32	13.28	15.99	19.89	25.97	16.05
.20	10.78	12.50	14.79	17.97	22.63	29.96	18.10
.25	11.73	13.68	16.30	19.96	25.38	33.95	20.16
.30	12.67	14.86	17.81	21.96	28,12	37.94	22.22
.35	13.62	16.04	19.32	23.95	30.86	41.93	24.28
.40	14.56	17.21	20.83	25.94	33.60	45.92	26.34

Table II.2 (continued)

$D \rightarrow$	.90	.91	.92	.93	.94	.95	Unweighted Average
R $\downarrow$	$I = 0.35$						
.05	7.52	8.50	9.76	11.44	13.80	17.32	11.39
.10	8.55	9.78	11.40	13.60	16.77	21.65	13.62
.15	9.57	11.06	13.03	15.76	19.74	25.97	15.86
.20	10.60	12.33	14.67	17.92	22.71	30.29	18.09
.25	11.62	13.61	16.30	20.08	25.68	34.61	20.32
.30	12.64	14.89	17.94	22.24	28.65	38.94	22.55
.35	13.67	16.17	19.57	24.40	31.62	43.26	24.78
.40	14.69	17.45	21.21	26.57	34.59	47.58	27.01
R $\downarrow$	$I = 0.40$						
.05	7.08	8.01	9.23	10.85	13.13	16.56	10.81
.10	8.16	9.36	10.95	13.13	16.27	21.12	13.16
.15	9.24	10.71	12.68	15.40	19.40	25.68	15.52
.20	10.32	12.06	14.40	17.68	22.53	30.24	17.87
.25	11.40	13.41	16.13	19.96	25.67	34.80	20.23
.30	12.48	14.76	17.85	22.24	28.80	39.36	22.58
.35	13.56	16.10	19.58	24.51	31.93	43.92	24.93
.40	14.64	17.45	21.30	26.79	35.07	48.48	27.29

Table II.3

Values of ΣB for ranges of I from .05 → .40
R from .05 → .40
D unweighted average .90 → .95

R	.05	.10	.15	.20	.25	.30	.35	.40
I $\downarrow$								
.05	13.86	14.32	14.79	15.25	15.72	16.18	16.65	17.12
.10	13.57	14.45	15.33	16.22	17.10	17.98	18.86	19.75
.15	13.23	14.48	15.73	16.98	18.23	19.48	20.73	21.98
.20	12.84	14.41	15.98	17.55	19.12	20.69	22.26	23.83
.25	12.41	14.25	16.09	17.93	19.77	21.60	23.44	25.28
.30	11.93	13.99	16.05	18.10	20.16	22.22	24.28	26.34
.35	11.39	13.62	15.86	18.09	20.32	22.55	24.78	27.01
.40	10.81	13.16	15.52	17.87	20.23	22.58	24.93	27.29

Values in this table are from the last columns in Table II/2 A–D

Particular points worth noting are the following:

1. For all values of D and I, the higher R is the higher total benefit is; furthermore the quantitative significance of R is very substantial. In other words, getting the value of R up is as important a policy objective as increasing I to get the economy to as high a value of total benefit as possible.

2. Except for very low values of R, especially combined with bottom values of D, increasing I increases the value of total benefit — but progressively less so as I gets larger. This is perhaps seen more clearly from Table II.3, which shows unweighted average values for total benefit in terms of I and R for all the values of D from .90 to .95. The main implication is that the higher the value of R the more worth while it is to push up the value of I for almost all values of D.

3. Putting the same point another way, the best approach to increasing values of total benefit is to raise I and R simultaneously, as the cumulative effect of raising them both together is more than twice that of raising either one without the other.

4. Although it is quite clear from the table that higher values of D, implying lower rates of discount of the future, lead to higher values of total benefit, as one would expect, it is also very interesting to note that the policy implications from the tables for increasing total benefit hardly alter over the relevant areas whatever value of D is chosen within the band .90 - .95. In other words the prescription from the tables for this band of values for D is that it is always worth pushing up the value of I and R. However, it can also be seen from the tables that with lower rates of discount than 5%, giving D a value of more than .95, the amount of reinvestment advocated gets higher and higher whatever the value of R, and below a value of .90 the amount of investment advocated starts to fall off until even reasonable values of R will not stop a policy prescription of rapid disinvestment. The fact that neither of these policies accords with common sense, whereas the policy prescriptions for all the values between .90 and .95 — this band being chosen by common sense — consistently advocate a higher rate of reinvestment than is current at least in the U.K. strongly suggests that we ignore this prescription at our peril.[16]

Tests on the Strength and Significance of the Assumptions made in the Model

Before we move on to fitting other objectives into the model we have developed there are three more investigations which must be made into what has been done so far. One is to relax the assumption made at the beginning of the model development that both the population and the labour force remain static; the second is to measure the significance of the assumption made about d; and the third is to test the importance of the assumption made that investment has a one year gestation period.

With regard to changes in the size of the population and the labour force there are two special cases to be considered, one being a static population and an increasing labour force, and the other is a rising population and a static labour force. When these two cases have been evaluated they can then be combined together to produce an effect on total benefit which allows for the effect of both together. Incidentally the consequences of a reduction in the size of either the population or the labour force is not dealt with here in detail on the grounds that neither is very likely, but the effects could easily be worked out by the same process used below.

Let us consider first the case where the population is static and the labour force is growing by x% p.a. Other things being equal this will lead to an extra increase in output next year of rather less than x% p.a., typically about .75x% p.a. using the same yardstick as on page 41. Let us call this y% p.a. The terms for the series for toal benefit on all the usual assumptions now become:

$$B_0 = C$$
$$B_1 = CD \frac{100 + y}{100} C \frac{100 + y}{100}$$

For the ease of writing let us say that

$$\frac{100 + y}{100} = z$$

Then
$$B_0 = C$$
$$B_1 = CDz + CIRDz$$
$$B_2 = CD^2 z^2 + 2\, CIRD^2 z^2$$

and
$$= \frac{C}{1 - Dz} + \frac{CIRDz}{(1 - Dz)^2}$$

Let us now consider the second case where the labour force is static and the population is rising. Now first we must decide whether there is anything here to be considered at all, because if the population rises by a small percentage, say 1%, then income per head will fall by 1% but the number of people enjoying an income will have risen by 1%. It could therefore be argued that since the rise involved was so small, factor d could be ignored, as the benefit being obtained remained exactly the same since the decrease per head was offset by the increased number enjoying it. However this is not a very satisfactory procedure, because surely what we ought to do is to look at this problem from the point of view of each individual in society and aggregate up from there, in which case, of course, a rise in population with a static labour force will, other things being equal, lead to a proportional reduction in benefit per head. Adopting this latter course as being the more realistic, let us investigate the case where the labour force remains static and the population rises by s% p.a. The terms of the series for total benefit now become:

$$B_0 = C$$

$$B_1 = CD \frac{100 - s}{100} + C \frac{100 - s}{100} IRD$$

For the ease of exposition let us say that

$$\frac{100 - s}{100} = t$$

Then $B_0 = C$

$$B_1 = CDt + CIRDt$$

$$B_2 = CD^2 t^2 + CIRD^2 t^2$$

and $$B = \frac{C}{(1 - Dt)} + \frac{CIRDt}{(1 - Dt)^2}$$

From these workings it is not difficult to see that the effect made by rising work forces and populations in each case is the same as is made by altering the value of D. With the sort of increases in population which have been experienced in some countries the effect on D would be pretty marked, but in most developed countries, and particularly in the U.K. over the next few years, the alterations in the size of both population and labour force are likely to be less than 1% p.a.[17] A further point to be noticed is that the effect of a rising labour force is to increase D, while the effect of a rising population is to depress D.

Now in practice a growing population and a growing labour force tend to go together, so that the two effects on D which we are investigating tend, at least in part, to cancel each other out. The orders of magnitude involved can be gauged by considering the case of a simultaneous rise in population and labour force of 2% p.a. From the workings above it can soon be seen that this rate of increase would give t a value of .98 and z a value of approximately 1.015. Multiplying these two together to get the combined effect gives a value of about .995. A factor of this sort is going to make relatively little difference to D, and in the case of the U.K. the difference would be considerably smaller still. Thus the effect on total benefit would be minimal — provided both population and labour force do move together; otherwise the difference would be considerably larger. However, as regards policy prescription even in this last case there would not be much alteration unless b and z diverged widely, since, as we have already seen, the whole model is not very sensitive to D as far as prescription is concerned.

We must now turn to testing the significance of the assumptions made earlier on about factor d — the effect of the declining marginal utility of income. It will be recalled that after investigation of the available evidence the conclusion reached was that the most satisfactory way of dealing with this problem was to assume that equal proportional increases in real income led to equal increases in benefit — i.e. a £200 a year increase in real income to the £2,000 p.a. man gave the same increase in benefit as an increase of £100 a year increase to the £1,000 p.a. man. Let us now make the assumption that we were wrong in thinking that these gains in benefit were equal and see what effect this would have. Writing the usual series of terms for total benefit we have:

$$B_0 = C$$
$$B_1 = CD + CIRD$$
$$B_2 = CD + 2CIRD$$

The fact that the value of the second term for B_2 is twice what it was for B_1 is derived from our assumption that equal proportional increases in income give equal increases in benefit. Let us now suppose that this assumption was wrong and that to allow for this a further factor p has to be introduced so that the second term for B_1 becomes $CpIRD$, and for B_2 $2CpIRD$. It will be noted that we are assuming at the moment that whatever value factor p may have — i.e. more or less than unity — it stays constant from year to year, but even this assumption will be removed shortly.

The terms of the series for total benefit now become:

$$B_0 = C$$
$$B_1 = CD + CpIRD$$
$$B_2 = CD^2 + 2CpIRD^2$$
$$B_n = CD^n + nCpIRD^n$$

and
$$\Sigma B = \frac{C}{(1-D)} + \frac{CpIRD}{(1-D)^2}$$

Now the sensitivity of values of total benefit to changes in the value of p is best seen by inspecting the respective values of each of the two terms on the right hand side. Let us therefore multiply both terms by $(1-D)/C$; they then become:

$$1 \text{ and } \frac{pIRD}{(I-D)}$$

Inspection of this ratio shows that the value of total benefit is more sensitive to p when I, R and D all have high values; values of .40, .40 and .95 respectively give a ratio of 1:3.04. However these values, particularly for I and R, are much higher than we are likely to light upon in practice; more reasonable ones would be respectively .25, .25 and .95 giving a ratio of 1:1.19, or .25, .25 and .90 giving a ratio of 1:.56. In sum, for the sort of figures we shall be dealing with a ratio of 1:1 would be a rather high middle figure implying that a 1% error in p produces an error of ½% in the value for total benefit.

Turning now to values for I_{opt} we find that the new term for I_{opt} allowing for p is:

$$I_{opt} = \frac{RDp - 1 + D}{2RDp} = \frac{1}{2}\left\{1 - \frac{(1-D)}{RDp}\right\}$$

With values for R and D which are of the order of magnitude we shall be dealing with, we find that the value of $(1-D)/RD$ comes out as follows:

R	D	$\dfrac{(1-D)}{RD}$
.40	.95	.1316
.40	.90	.2778
.25	.95	.2105
.25	.90	.4444
.10	.95	.5263
.10	.90	1.1111

It can be seen from these figures that unless very low values of R are combined with bottom values for D a 1% change in p produces a change of less than ¼% in I_{opt}. This is so because a value of .5 for $(1-D)/RD$, giving I_{opt} a value of $½(1 - 5p)$ alters by ¼% for every 1% change in the value of p, and only bottom values of R and D together give values of $(1 - D)/RD$ of more than .5.

The general conclusion to be reached therefore about factor d is that we could afford to be quite widely wrong about the way in which the marginal utility of incomes falls without the results of the analysis being much affected. This is particularly so because factor p has been measured as the extent to which factor d does not work in the way originally posited, when changes in income per head are in fact fairly small — of the order of size which can be achieved by one year's growth in the economy. While it may stretch the imagination to assume that a £200 a year rise increases the satisfaction of the £2,000 p.a. man by exactly the same amount as a £100 a year rise to the £1,000 p.a. man, these are not the sorts of magnitude of difference with which p is concerned. It seems much more credible to think that £200 to the £2,000 p.a. man increases satisfaction by the same amount as £210 to the man earning £2,100. Thus there are good reasons for thinking that at worst factor p is not likely to be of the order of more than 1% or 2% either side of unity, and on this basis the implications for the model are barely perceptible within the margins of error we are working with anyway. And furthermore, even if p was not a constant factor, i.e. it varied from year to year, it would still not make much difference because early values for p are, by inspection, much more important than later ones because of factor D. Thus the argument that p will eventually be less than unity because the world will reach economic saturation point may well be sound, but the effect on present values of total benefit is completely negligible.

Finally, we must check whether our assumption that all investment has a gestation period of one year is a strong one. In particular we must check whether it is reasonable to use the national income statistics to obtain values for R, bearing in mind that all investment does not necessarily take one year to mature, and in view of all the assumptions which have now been made about D and d. To investigate this point let us consider the case where the average gestation period is two years and not one, and to make the situation as clear as possible let us suppose that the economy increases in two year steps instead of the one year steps which we have been considering up till now. The series for total benefit now becomes:

$$
\begin{aligned}
B_0 &= C \\
B_1 &= CD \\
B_2 &= CD^2 + CIRD^2 \\
B_3 &= CD^3 + CIRD^3 \\
B_4 &= CD^4 + 2CIRD^4 \\
B_5 &= CD^5 + 2CIRD^5 \\
B_6 &= CD^6 + 3CIRD^6
\end{aligned}
$$

Without proof in the text, though this can be found in Appendix A, the sum of this double series of terms is:

$$
\frac{C}{(1 - D)} + \frac{D^2 CIR(1 + D)}{(1 - D^2)^2}
$$

The question which must now be asked is: if the average gestation period for investment is two years and not one, what bias is introduced into our model by the fact that there is twice the waiting time before investment comes on stream than we have posited up till now, even though the eventual consumption flow from this investment remains the same? The answer is that R would have to alter in such a way as to make the total benefit of the new two year step equal to the original total benefit. Again without proof, which will be found in Appendix A, to make the two values the same, the value of the two year step R — say R' — would have to be such that:

$$
R' = R \frac{(1 + D)}{D}
$$

The implication of this analysis is that the danger of bias in using national income statistics for R is very small. Even if our estimate of a one year gestation period is out by a factor of two, so that the average gestation period was two years, the bias introduced would be a function of how far $(1 + D)/D$ differed from 2. If $D = .95$ the value of $(1 + D)/D = 2.0526$, and if $D = .90$ it is 2.111. Thus, even assuming that the average gestation period was two years and not one, the bias involved would be of the order of 2½%-5%. However, since a great deal of investment has a shorter period than one year, the chance of the average being very far away from one year seems to be fairly small. This point is particularly forceful when it is remembered that with substantial investment projects with a long period before they begin to pay off not all the sacrifice involved in the investment is made at the beginning; it is made cumulatively as the investment projects work their way towards completion. It seems therefore safe to ignore any bias which could be introduced from gestation periods for investment differing from one year.

This point should not be confused with another really vital one about the period of gestation of one piece of investment as against another, which amazingly seems to have escaped the attention of every commentator on investment appraisal. As has been stressed time after time in this book, what is really important about investment is the cumulative quality it has for producing more output in the future. This output is not available until the investment comes on stream because it is only then that it starts producing its social rate of return, from which more savings can be made for more investment in the future. While investment is gestating it is normal for it to bear an opportunity cost in the form of interest, but this is just a transfer payment — nothing to do with actual increased output. However it is a sobering fact that investment with a one year pay off period is more than twice as valuable in contributing to increased output and growth generally as investment with a two year gestation period, assuming that in each case the social rate of return is the same once the investment is on stream. The implications for policy prescription from this analysis are exceedingly far reaching and will be discussed in the next chapter, but the effect on investment appraisal of projects such as the Concorde supersonic aeroplane — with a gestation period of something like ten years — can be imagined.

Perhaps the point should be restressed that national income statistics measure the average value of R, allowing for the fact that the contribution of some investment to producing new output is much quicker than others, and also for the fact that some investment has a much lower capital/output ratio than others — i.e. its contribution to the overall potential value of R is greater. The difference in effect on R of long and short gestation periods can be used as a policy weapon for raising R; it does not mean that national income statistics cannot be used to measure the average.

Part 3   Other Policy Objectives

Procedure for dealing with Other Policy Objectives

We must now turn to the other policy objectives which up till now have not been considered and fit them into the model we are building up. It will be recalled that the main desiderata which we still have to investigate are the following:
  - the desirability of a stable balance of payments with fixed or floating rates of exchange
  - price stability as against varying degrees of inflation
  - unemployment and pressure of demand
  - income and wealth distribution

The procedure to be adopted in each case is to see whether achievement or otherwise of these desiderata by themselves affect total benefit and then to see whether they have any secondary affects because they influence other factors which in turn affect total benefit. Let us deal with them in turn.

The Balance of Payments

First let us ask whether it is a sensible policy to have as a policy objective the running of a balance of payments surplus or deficit overall on both current and capital accounts together. As regards a surplus this must take the form of accumulating monetary reserves in the form of either gold, which earns no interest at all, or S.D.R.'s, which carry very low rates of interest, or lending money back to debtor countries at rates which, net of inflation, are also very low if not negative, and which certainly do not even begin to show a return anything like the social rate of return on domestic investment. Probably the most sensible way of treating surpluses of this sort is to treat them as consumption foregone, and so as reducing C and thus total benefit, at least as long as surpluses are not required to pay a country's way out of a genuinely insolvent situation. The reduction in total benefit is offset to some extent by monetary (rather than social) returns on consumption foregone (interest on loans from abroad) and also by the fact that surpluses could be run down in the future so raising benefit, although any such gains would be subject to factor D. Allowing for these two factors we will assume that current total benefit should be reduced by half of the ratio between the size of the surplus on current account and the value of current consumption. When viewed in this light the policy pursued by the Germans over the last ten years during which their reserves have risen by a very large sum while total consumption has been a rather low proportion of the national income does not look very attractive.

Per contra running a deficit on current and capital account together, as the U.K. did for most of the 60's is a rational policy, or would be if it were possible to get away with it indefinitely. However, the scope for a policy of this sort is strictly circumscribed by the patience of debtor countries, and is clearly not a serious possibility on any scale for any length of time, although it is obviously feasible for comparatively short tiding over periods. The fairly straightforward conclusion we arrive at, therefore, about the balance of payments as an objective is that taking one year with another one should try to avoid deficits, but one should also try and avoid surpluses. In particular, the large surpluses piled up by countries such as Germany should be avoided at all costs. By the same token no effort should be made to liquidate existing funded debts, such as the sterling balances, although this is, of course, not an argument against exchanging them for some other form of long term liability such as to the I.M.F.

Is there a case for distinguishing between capital and current accounts? In theory the answer must be yes. If a balance of trade deficit could be offset permanently by an inflow of capital which is earning only a private and not a social rate of return for its foreign investors, then total benefit in the domestic country would clearly be pushed up. The dangers of this policy are, first, that relying on net foreign investment on a very large scale to keep foreign payments balanced exposes the domestic economy rather more than most people would like to the whims of foreign investors, and, second, beyond a certain point there may be political difficulties if larger sections of the domestic economy become controlled by foreign companies. This is a policy which is therefore worth pursuing, but with caution.

On the other hand there is no doubt whatever that the policy of running a balance of trade surplus to finance capital exports is likely to depress domestic total benefit. Of course there are other considerations involved if the capital exports are going to under-developed countries, though total benefit is still affected just as much, but it is simply not true that most British capital exports go to under-developed countries;

most of them go to those already developed.[18] There is partly an accounting reason why this is so: profits made by companies operating abroad owned by residents of the domestic economy show in the national accounts as property income from abroad; however, if any of the profits made abroad are retained there in the businesses where they were made to be used for expansion they then reappear in the national accounts as investment overseas. Clearly there is a limit beyond which it is not worth starving existing overseas investments of cash for expansion, but it would be more rational to try to persuade such companies to raise money for expansion where possible in the country where the expansion was taking place, and, of course, none of these considerations applies to new investment. Certainly the type of balance of trade surplus advocated by the Radcliffe Committee would be highly undesirable. The problem with investing overseas is simply this: the private rate of return may be higher than in the domestic economy, but the vast proportion of the social rate of return remains overseas and is not available to the domestic economy.

We must now turn to the question of exchange rates and inquire whether there is any policy in this area which would improve total benefit. It might appear that the best policy would be to have as overvalued a currency as possible in order to achieve the best possible terms of trade. This is a commonly held view but, as the U.K. has found over the last twenty years, this policy has disastrous side effects as a result of the deflation required to keep the exchange in balance, and anyway, as we shall see shortly, there is no good reason to believe that having an overvalued currency necessarily improves the terms of trade. The current policy goal is to try to get the value of sterling in line with world currencies generally, and this is certainly better than having it overvalued, in so far that less deflation is required. But why not carry this line of advance a bit further and aim to have sterling undervalued? There would be practical difficulties in getting this policy accepted by other countries which we shall investigate later; at this stage let us confine ourselves to the theoretical pros and cons. The main advantage is that it may be possible to engineer a considerable improvement in investment prospects by having an undervalued currency — a point which we shall return to later. The two main theoretical disadvantages are first that there may be a deterioration in total benefit as a result of worsening terms of trade, and second that there is a substantial danger of more inflation caused by rising import prices. The real costs of inflation will be dealt with later, but the effects on total benefit of changes in the terms of trade and the balance of payments must be dealt with now.

Exchange Rates and the Terms of Trade

To make the point at issue as simple as possible let us consider an economy with a net national product of £1,000m, of which 30% is both imported and exported — roughly the ratio for the U.K. — and let us assume that before any changes are made the external accounts are in balance, i.e. with £300m of exports and imports valued in domestic currency. Let us now consider what happens if there is a devaluation of say 20%. Two things are bound to happen: both import and export prices are bound to rise in terms of the domestic currency, and fall in terms of external currencies. The critical point is whether the rise in import prices is larger than the rise in export prices. If it is the terms of trade worsen and there is a real cost to be borne, but if they both rise together there is no cost at all, and indeed if export prices rose more than import prices there would actually be a gain to the domestic economy. The orders of magnitude of these gains and losses are calculated as follows: supposing the 20% devaluation led to a 15% rise in import prices, foreign suppliers absorbing the other 5%, and a 10% rise in export prices, involving a 10% cut in export prices in external currency. There would then be a 5% deterioration in the terms of trade and the cost would be 5% times the proportion (0.3) of the national income involved in foreign trade — i.e. 1.5%. B would be reduced by this proportion, hence so would all the terms in the series of ΣB and thus the value for total benefit. The general case therefore is that the effect on total benefit of devaluation is to alter total benefit by the alteration in terms of trade times the proportion of the national income involved with foreign trade.

There is a further point to be made: when devaluation takes place there is bound to be an increase in the volume of exports and a reduction in the volume of imports. However it does not follow from this that the balance of payments position will improve. If large price changes made very little difference to the volumes involved the balance of payment situation could actually deteriorate. In the example above if both import and export volumes remained exactly as they were before devaluation, or only changed very slightly, imports would rise by £45m but exports receipts would only rise by £30m leading to a deficit of £15m. However, this case is not at all likely and the evidence available suggests that the elasticity of demand for exports at least is fairly high, in which case a reduction in export prices in external currency of 1% leads to a volume increase of considerably more than 1% so that the total value of exports goes up in terms of external currencies. Of course it always goes up in terms of the domestic devalued currency. The general condition for the balance of payments improving as a result of devaluation is that the elasticities of demand for imports and exports together should be more than unity. Assuming for the moment that the elasticity constraint is one which can be ignored because the elasticities are adequately large, and assuming that there is at least some deterioration in the terms of trade as a result of devaluation, whether it is worth devaluing or not turns on whether the gains to total benefit, particularly via increasing values of R and I caused by better domestic economic conditions resulting from having a relatively undervalued currency, offset the reduction in total benefit which may be the immediate consequence of devaluation. It should be noted that not a very large increase in I and R would be necessary to offset the real costs of even a fairly substantial worsening of the terms of trade. Perhaps it is worth remarking at this stage that neither the 1949 nor the 1967 U.K. devaluation appears to have altered the terms of trade appreciably at all.[19]

The general conclusion is that there is not much direct scope for increasing total benefit via either balance of payments or exchange rate policy, but that getting these policies right has a great deal to do with allowing other objectives to be achieved. Furthermore there appear to be reasons for believing that exchange rate policy could be used not just as a way of balancing transactions across the exchanges but in a much more purposive manner. If it is true that possible worsening terms of trade have a manageably small effect on total benefit, that the problems of inflation as a result of devaluation turn out to be surmountable, and the practical difficulties involved in getting other countries to agree to us having a more undervalued currency can be overcome, then it could be that exchange rate policy could have a very important role indeed to play in pushing up total benefit by making an export led investment boom a practical possibility. However, there is a lot more analysis and quantification to be done before such a policy can be accepted.

Before leaving the subject of the balance of payments and exchange rate policy something must be said about the question of fixed rates of exchange, crawling pegs, freely floating and managed rates. From what has already been said and what is to follow it will be clear that any arrangements which lead to deflation to maintain fixed parities are definitely inclined to cause extremely depressed values of total benefit, and are therefore to be avoided; however, one's attitude to fixed parities inevitably turns on whether one's own parity is above or below par, and it is surely no coincidence that those countries with fixed undervalued currencies, such as Japan, have been most reluctant to see the present system altered. However, this is a very selfish beggar-my-neighbour policy which ought to be exposed more widely for what it is. Of the alternatives to fixed parities, crawling peg type arrangements get over the problem of the rigidity of fixed parities but preclude exchange rate policy being used in the purposive manner hinted at earlier on. Much the same can be said of freely floating rates, apart from the fact that rightly or wrongly no government is ever going to allow its currency rate to be determined wholly by a free market however desirable this may be on theoretical grounds. Managed floating is the most immediately practical alternative to fixed parities, perhaps combined with at least threatened devluations to keep the rate in the right place and is the one which the analysis in this book would favour, albeit with the proviso that there may well be much greater scope than has been appreciated up to now for using exchange rate policy to achieve growth without incurring insupportable burdens in other directions.

Stable Prices and Inflation

Let us now turn to stable prices, as against inflation, as a policy objective. Several reasons have been put forward for preferring stable prices to inflation and we must investigate these in turn to see what effect each of these arguments against inflation has on total benefit.

First it is argued that inflation leads to a worsening distribution of income, and in particular that inflation hits those on fixed incomes, the poor and unsophisticated. It also tends to favour the recipients of profits, dividends and rent as against the wage and salary earners, and favours the militant well organised trade unionists as against those who are either poorly organised or not organised at all. This sounds a formidable catalogue of demerits, but on further investigation into what has actually happened it turns out that the situation is rather different. What appears to be the case is that increasing rates of inflation have all the effects mentioned above, but that steady rates of inflation do not because everybody gradually adjusts to them. Furthermore almost all these results of inflation are much more marked before taking into account the effects of progressive income tax, capital gains taxes such as they are, and transfer payments, all of which substantially diminish the impact which even increasing rates of inflation have on the distribution of wealth and income. A much more valid test of the effects of inflation on income distribution is provided by inspection of the actual post tax distribution of income, after allowing for the receipt of all social security benefits. Comparing distributions for different years during the quarter century since the end of World War II should provide conclusive evidence as to whether inflation of the order we have had in Britain during this period does or does not lead inevitably to a more uneven distribution of income. Unfortunately, the evidence is not as clear cut as one would hope owing to the extraordinary difficulties involved in relating the only relevant sources of information, such as Inland Revenue statistics, back from income units to individuals. Depending on the way the available data is worked the indications are sometimes that the post tax and social security distribution of incomes has got slightly more uneven, and sometimes that it has got a little less so, but there is no substantial evidence to show any marked change in either direction. There is certainly no evidence that inflation has caused any substantial change in the final distribution of income, and indeed this is not really surprising when one considers the 'catching up' argument which is so frequently advanced to justify wage and social security increases; this is always an argument which attracts public sympathy. It may well be the case that many people would regret that the distribution has not become more nearly equal, but viewed in this light it is difficult to see that inflation can be blamed for the fact that this movement towards equality has not taken place. We must therefore conclude that the effect of inflation, over a reasonable time period at least, on total benefit via income distribution is minimal.[20]

The second argument against inflation is that it leads to misallocation of resources because some prices are more inflexible and amenable to pressure than others, particularly from the government. The consequence is that too many resources are deployed into areas where demand is excessive because of underpricing, the whole public sector being generally cited as being the worst offender; indeed it has been suggested that the entire output of the public sector is probably undercharged for by a factor of some 5-10% compared with private sector prices.[21] Furthermore it has been clear for some time that a very considerable degree of distortion has appeared in the accounts of industry and commerce, in both the public and the private sector, as a result of conventional accounting practice whereby assets are written off at historic and not replacement costs. As a result capital consumption is certainly understated, the implication being that net investment, as shown in the national accounts, may well be considerably lower than actually appears. This is a point we have already discussed on page 40. Now there are really two separate issues involved in these contentions: on the one hand is the question of whether the allocation of resources in real terms as a result of inflation is going so far adrift as to lower R, and on the other is a matter of whether the book-keeping techniques used are measuring accurately what is going on. As regards the straight question of misallocation of resources there seems little doubt that some has happened, though it is not clear that very much is attributable to inflation rather than other factors. And in any case is the answer to this problem necessarily less inflation, or a more rational policy by the government in letting prices in the public sector rise in line with those in the private sector? And at the bottom, was the government really holding down prices in the public sector because of worries about inflation *per se*, or were they in fact mainly worried about what inflation would do to the balance of payments? If this restraint were removed by more flexible exchange rate arrangements, would at least the larger part of the problem disappear? It seems likely. In sum, it does seem that there are dangers of at least some degree of misallocation of resources as long as there is any inflation at all particularly by underpricing the output of the public sector, although it is not clear that there is likely to be much more underpricing if inflation is greater because financial restraints begin to operate much more sharply on the public sector industries when they trade at a loss than when they are not making any profits. This provides an effective limit to the extent which underpricing can take place, and one which appears to have been already reached in several cases.

On the accounting problem the situation is somewhat different. Here we are not concerned with what is actually happening, but with our measurements of what is going on; not with total benefit itself, but with the accuracy with which we can measure it. Overall, the effect appears to be that I is overstated in the national income accounts, and C understated. However, the overall influence on total benefit is not likely to be very large simply because of the relationship between R and I. If I has been consistently overstated for the last ten years in the U.K. by 10%, then our measurement for R will be understated by an exactly similar amount; inspection of the expression for ΣB shows that the net effect of these changes is to leave the value for total benefit unaltered. As far as prediction of the future is concerned any understatement for R is a matter of considerable importance, though we shall find that the values of R alter by much larger amounts than 10% over quite short periods of time. In any case, some allowance for overstatement of I has really been allowed for in the way we dealt with the net/gross investment problem on page 40.

The argument that inflation causes difficulties with the balance of payments, at least if inflation in the domestic economy is at a greater rate than in the economies of trade rivals, is one which is wearisome in its familiarity. However this is really not so much an argument against inflation as for a more rational exchange rate policy, and if this were implemented so that any excess of inflation in the domestic economy could be offset by a corresponding reduction in the external value of the domestic currency this problem would disappear. Certainly in terms of total benefit, if a sensible exchange rate policy is pursued, there need be no effect at all from inflation on this score.

A further argument against inflation is that it may lead to hyper-inflation, the situation which occurred in Germany after both World Wars, in Hungary in 1947 and in China in 1949. Clearly at some rate of inflation the financial and monetary system will stop working at all, and at a much earlier point it will start working very inefficiently, and total benefit would be very seriously affected. However, one of the remarkable things to note about the economic history of the world during the last twenty years is that there has not been one single case of hyper-inflation, although very high rates of inflation have been experienced. In some countries in South America, and in Indonesia, annual doubling of the price level has not been uncommon,[22] and yet the currency has not lost its use, and all things considered the performance of the economies where these very high rates of inflation have been experienced has been surprisingly good — at least in the sense that the difficulties they may have experienced are mainly attributable to more obviously pressing problems than those caused by inflation. The experience of these countries certainly suggests that the risk of a mature economy such as the United Kingdom suffering from hyper-inflation is very remote. Furthermore the fact that those countries which have had very high rates of inflation do not seem to have had their economic progress hindered all that much by this state of affairs lends further support to the view that the effects of misallocation of resources in the U.K. cannot be all that great as a result of the very modest inflation we have experienced in the past, or are likely to experience in the future, judged by other parts of the world.

Finally, there is the argument that inflation is unpleasant because it is awkward having prices changing. There is no doubt at all that everyone finds rising prices very irritating, and that this process is very unpopular. However closer inspection shows that it is not prices changing which is unpopular, but prices rising and thus eroding away the effects of wage and salary increases, to which no recipient ever raises any objection whatever. Nor do we find those who put prices up bemoaning their misfortune in getting more for their goods or services. All this argument boils down to is the obvious truth that people like the part of the inflationary spiral which helps them — which for the vast mass of the people takes the form of increased wages and salaries — and dislike the part which wholly or partially removes this advantage from them — i.e. price increases. There is very little evidence that people are greatly worried about prices changing *per se*.

There is, however, one way in which inflation may have costs which are material deriving from the sheer awkwardness of prices changing, and this is via the adjustment process particularly as regards trade union claims for higher wages which may lead to strikes. There is no doubt, of course, that trade unions do often strike for higher wages, although many strikes are not about wages at all but about working conditions, but it is not at all clear that inflation makes the chances of strikes all that much greater. If there were more wage claims because of inflation the situation would be different, but in fact everyone now has got used to having some sort of a rise in money terms every year, and the argument is about what the size of the rise should be, not whether there should be one at all. While more inflationary conditions may make this size determination a little more difficult, there does not seem to be any evidence to suggest that there are likely to be appreciably more strikes caused by one level inflation rather than another.

Having now examined all the arguments currently put forward against inflation, what general conclusions emerge regarding both the direct and indirect effects of inflation on the measurement of total benefit? There are two ways in which total benefit can be affected, via C and via R. With regard to C it would have to be shown that the satisfaction derived from the output of the economy would have to be reduced simply because the prices at which it was being sold were altering. In all the arguments which we have examined against inflation there does not seem to be a shred of evidence to support this view and we can only therefore conclude that C remains unaltered, given the magnitude of the output of the economy, at least within the range of inflation that we are likely to be dealing with.[23] The other way in which total benefit can be affected is if R is reduced because of inflation, and there is some evidence that this is likely to happen. It certainly will happen if deflationary policies are used to deal with balance of payments problems caused by inflation, but this problem can be overcome by more flexible exchange rate policies. The other point of substance concerned the misallocation of resources caused by inflation. We found some difficulty in quantifying how substantial this would be and the fact that other countries which had very much larger rates of inflation did not seem to have their economic performance impaired very much in consequence lends support to the view that the extent to which misallocation of resources caused by inflation cannot be very substantial. It is also noteworthy that Japan, which as we shall see later has the highest value of R of any country, also has had a consistently higher rate of inflation than most other developed countries.[24] While not ignoring altogether the effect of inflation on reducing R, therefore, we cannot accept that any reduction would be very great.

We therefore arrive at the rather surprising conclusion that a policy goal of stable prices or minimal amounts of inflation does not have very much to recommend it at all — provided arrangements are made to stop inflation upsetting the balance of payments. A rate of inflation of 10% or so appears to have very little effect on total benefit. This is a very important conclusion because if it is accepted then one major potential restraint on the achievement of other objectives is removed.

Unemployment

Unemployment is normally taken to refer to people who are out of work, and we would certainly want to pay full attention to this aspect of the problem. However it is not only people who are unemployed in deflationary conditions; capital equipment, particularly in manu-facturing industry, is also shut down completely or else under-utilised.

There is a reduction in current benefit from both these sources below that which could be obtained if they were both used to the full. We shall therefore consider unemployment of people and capital equipment separately, but in estimating the reduction in benefit which registered unemployment reflects we will combine together the loss of benefit caused by having people out of work with the loss of benefit caused by under-utilisation of capital.[25]

Let us consider first the reduction in benefit caused by having people unemployed. Since roughly 75% of all factor rewards go to labour it will be apparent that the costs of having people out of work are very heavy. Furthermore, being unemployed is a sickening and humiliating experience for anyone, and if a certain level of output is achieved with a substantial measure of unemployment then it simply cannot be said that the economy is providing the same level of benefit as it would if exactly the same output has been achieved with full employment. Furthermore the benefit being obtained from the economy is sub-optimal when labour and capital resources are standing idle, because more output would be obtained without any additional cost to the economy by bringing them into service. While the qualititive position is clear, quantification in this area is not at all easy for at least three reasons. First, the labour force is not homogeneous; second, it is difficult to assess exactly to what extent the percentage of the total labour force which is unemployed is a measure of the degree to which labour is being involuntarily under-utilised; and third, it is even more difficult to measure the reduction in total benefit caused by the social distress of those who are out of work. However, some attempt can be made at least to get at the orders of magnitude involved.

If the labour force were entirely homogeneous, there were no underemployment of those still in work, and those in receipt of the dole were just as happy with their incomes as they would have been if the money had been earned, then it would not be difficult to calculate the reduction in benefit from unemployment. It would be labour's share of factor rewards times the percentage unemployed — i.e. the reduction in total benefit from every 1% of the labour force which was unemployed would be approximately 0.75%. It is the adjustments to this figure caused by lack of homogeneity in the labour force, unemployment of labour being a symptom of much more widespread underemployment, and the social distress caused by being out of work, which make quantification difficult. Let us deal with these adjustments in turn.

Data about what those who are unemployed would be earning if they were in work is, understandably, not easy to come by, but it is generally recognised that the average earning power of those out of work is considerably lower than for those in employment. Inspection of the distribution of wages and salaries suggests that the disparity could be anywhere between 25% and 50%, particularly when it is remembered that unemployed labour tends to be concentrated in low wage areas, although a countervailing argument here is that output per employee in work tends to be lower in these parts of the country as well. Perhaps an average figure of 33% would be as reasoned a guess as any. It is most regrettable that there seem to be no firm figures available anywhere upon which more accurate assessments could be made; indeed the true cost of unemployment generally is an area which cries out for more systematic investigation and research.

Again, when trying to assess the relationship between actual unemployment and underemployment of those in work there is little firm data on which to base an opinion, and one is pushed back to experience, common sense and guess work. One of the problems is that many people who would like to work do not bother to register as unemployed. Another problem is in distinguishing long term from short term effects. A temporary rise in unemployment will lead to short-lived work sharing practices, which will tend to be shed as soon as demand for labour picks up again, but long periods with high unemployment lead to institutionalised restrictive practices which are much harder to eradicate. If we exclude formal restrictive practices and concentrate on the short term and consider reductions in overtime, short time working, temporary over-manning etc. and add in unregistered unemployment, it seems difficult to avoid the conclusion that the loss of output from underemployment is very substantial. Evidence from Britain recently, however, suggests that nowadays employers are much more inclined to discharge redundant labour than they were, indicating that the ratio between unemployment and underemployment is probably rising. The very rapid rises in productivity in manufacturing industry in Britain recently are also a pointer in the same direction. Looking just at the short term it seems that the loss of output due to underemployment is something of the order of 50% — 100% of that lost because of unemployment of labour, though it must be admitted that this is only a guess. One would also hazard that a long period with very low unemployment would lead to much more efficient allocation of labour and would be a much better solvent of restrictive practices than any legislation or admonition. However, what we are concerned with in this section are the short terms gains and losses involved in changes in the number of the unemployed, rather than the long term gains from deploying a given proportion of the willing labour force more efficiently.

We are on even more difficult ground when trying to measure the social distress caused by unemployment in economic terms, although this is too important a consideration to be left out of the account. It is of considerable significance that of all the reasons for people being in receipt of assistance from the state only those receiving unemployment benefit are doing so purely because of the way the economy is managed. Whereas the social services are concerned with alleviating social distress of all kinds, better economic management has not got much to do with the solutions to most peoples' problems.[26] However we shall argue in the next Chapter that unemployment could be eradicated almost completely over a short period of time, and therefore the grief from unemployment should be counted into the balance in a way which is not appropriate for other social troubles.

How are we to measure this distress? Of all the problems tackled in this book this seems one of the most intractable, and the best solution seems to be simply to round up the costs of unemployment in terms of total benefit and hope that this copes with the problem in a fashion which is half adequate. Luckily we shall find that the prescription which is emerging from our model is towards policies that predicate full employment anyway, so we shall not be left with the cost of balancing off substantial unemployment against other gains.

It must be confessed that quantifying the costs of having people out of work in terms of total benefit has turned out to be very difficult, and at best all that can be hoped for is to arrive at the right order of magnitude rather than any exact measurement. On this basis the figures which emerge are as follows:

Assuming homogeneity of labour, no underemployment and no social distress from unemployment, 1% unemployment produces approximately 0.75% reduction in total benefit.

Adjusting for the fact that the earning capacity of those out of work is estimated at 1/3 less than those in work reduces the loss of total benefit to 0.50%.

Adjusting for the fact that unemployment only measures in part the extent to which labour is under-utilised in the short term increases the loss of benefit by a factor of somewhere around 50% - 100% raising the loss per 1% unemployment to between 0.75% and 1.0%.

Rounding up this figure to allow for the social distress caused by unemployment caused not by any personal incapacity but by demand deficiency, it seems that the ratio between percentage of registered unemployment and percentage loss of benefit due to unemployment of labour is of the order of one to one, although it may be more.

If one accepts that this procedure is giving approximately correct results, then it emerges that every 1% unemployment of labour reduces total benefit by 1%. However, we noted at the beginning of this section that unemployment of labour always tends to coincide with under-utilisation of capital equipment, particularly in manufacturing industry, so that there is a further heavy cost to be borne which is associated with the figures for unemployment as they are usually understood. There are two ways of getting at the order of magnitude of the loss of benefit caused by idle capital resources. In each case the first step is to establish the ratio between the amount of capacity made idle by deflation and the level of unemployment. Once this ratio has been obtained, estimates of lost benefit can be calculated either on the basis of factor reward splits, or on the basis of capital/output ratios.

Figures published on page 76 of *The Economist* on March 18th 1972 show the ratio fairly clearly between unemployment and under-utilisation of capacity. During the period between the beginning of 1966 and the end of 1971 unemployment increased from 1.6% to 4.1% while under-utilisation increased from about 11% to about 22%. While there may be some doubt as the exact accuracy of the under-utilisation percentages, the ratio is consistent enough over time to give a clear indication that for every 1% of registered unemployment about 4.4% of capital equipment is made idle. On a factor reward split of 75% to labour and 25% to capital it would appear that the reduction in benefit caused by under-utilisation of capital equipment, associated with a 1% level of registered unemployment, was 4.4% x 25%, which is 1.1%. A similar figure is arrived at by considering capital/output ratios. Anticipating the figures to be discussed in the next chapter, the actual capital/output ratio achieved by the British economy during the period 1961-70 was 5.65:1.[27] If the capital equipment made idle by deflation was of average capital/output ratio, the reduction in benefit associated with a 1% level of unemployment would be 4.4% divided by 5.65 which is just under .8%.

These results straddle a ratio of one to one for the loss of benefit from unemployed labour and under-utilised equipment. As we shall argue later that the capital/output ratios which form the basis of the second calculation are themselves considerably higher than would have been necessary with better policies in operation, it would seem fair to take the one to one ratio as being a reasonable minimum figure rather than a maximum. On this basis it now emerges that the total loss of benefit associated with every 1% of registered unemployment is of the order of 2% rather than 1%. Pending further research being undertaken to obtain a more accurate ratio we shall take this as being the correct one to adopt.

A policy objective of full employment therefore turns out to be one that is very important and fully vindicated by the Welfare Analysis which we have carried out. Compared with the insignificant contributions to total benefit caused by stable prices as against inflation, and fixed rates of exchange as against a more flexible approach to external parities, a policy of full employment is one whose contribution to total benefit is definite and substantial. It is a great pity that a more accurate measure of the gains and losses from varying rates of unemployment to total benefit could not be made, and it certainly seems that this is an area which needs to have much more research done on it.

There are two main dangers to the full employment policy advocated in the last paragraph. The first is that very low unemployment leads to inflation and the second is that it leads to bottlenecks. Regarding inflation, as there is definite evidence that full employment raises total benefit, and not much evidence that inflation pulls it down, we might be inclined to dismiss this argument as irrelevant. However, accepting that inflation does have some effect on R, and that values of total benefit are very sensitive to values of R, this approach is too cavalier. In any case, even if the gains to total benefit from less and less unemployment continue to offset losses by inflation, sooner or later the balance of advantage must swing the other way. However, where this point is reached would appear to depend very much on the circumstances of the case. Over the last twenty years in the U.K. the experience has been that boom conditions have been accompanied by rises in productivity which have absorbed wage increases better than slack conditions have, and that unemployment starts to fall about a year after the substantial gains in productivity start to be made, so that a further cushion against inflation is provided. Unfortunately, however, by this time trouble has started to loom up on the balance of payments front so that deflationary policies have to be imposed, bringing productivity gains to a complete halt, just at a time when everyone is getting used to substantial wage increases. A more potent recipe for inflationary wage claims could hardly be imagined, and this is one of the main reasons why reductions in unemployment have tended to be accompanied by inflation in the U.K. However, it might well be possible to by-pass these difficulties by engineering a boom which was not going to break, and which would then be able to continue to absorb wage increases without generating more inflation both because of productivity gains and because of reductions in unemployment. The prospects for a policy of this sort will be examined in much more detail in the next chapter; the point to be made here is that the connection between low unemployment figures and damagingly high rates of inflation may not be nearly so firm as many commentators have suggested it is.[28]

As regards the bottleneck argument that full employment implies such a high level of demand that the economy starts running very inefficiently because of shortages, again beyond a certain point one can see that this argument must have considerable force, but the crucial question is where the gains from a high pressure of demand, of which full employment is one, begin to be more than offset by losses from bottlenecks. This is a question which we will have to defer until the quantitative importance of a high level of demand has been established, but at this stage it can be said that the correlation between high values of R and a high level of demand is so marked that whatever the level of demand eventually decided upon as being appropriate, it is most unlikely to be such that any significant degree of unemployment of labour or capital resources would be likely to coincide with it.

The conclusion we therefore arrive at with regard to unemployment is that reductions in registered unemployment have a positive proportional effect on total benefit which is approximately twice as large as the reduction in the registered unemployment percentage achieved. Side effects of a full employment policy on total benefit, via inflation or excessive pressure of demand, may reduce the gains achieved, but are not likely to do so by very much unless unemployment reaches very low levels indeed. Because of the very beneficial effect on R of a high pressure of demand, with which full employment would coincide, combined with the relatively small adverse effects on R of inflation, which may not be made worse anyway, the chance of a conflict between full employment and other policy goals in the right environment is small. However, beyond a certain point, even with the best policy mix, the gains from extra reductions in employment would be offset by the results of inflation and bottlenecks, though experience from other countries, for example Germany, suggests that unemployment levels of only ½%-1% are perfectly feasible over long periods of time. This would seem to be a reasonable objective.

The Distribution of Income and Wealth

Finally we must deal with the questions of income and wealth distribution, and see how these can be fitted into the model we are developing. There are really two quite separate subjects here, and they are best dealt with in turn.

As regards income distribution there is no doubt that one of the conclusions which follows directly from the investigation which was carried out earlier into factor d is that there is a *prima facie* case for believing that benefit would be increased if there were a more equal distribution of income. Since the scope for altering the wages actually paid to people seems very limited, this objective has to be achieved through the tax system. However, as soon as redistribution in this way is proposed the argument is produced that high rates of direct taxation are a disincentive to effort, and thus reduce R, and also that particularly high rates of taxation on those with the highest incomes mulcts one of the major sources of saving, thus tending to reduce I. Reducing I and R reduces total benefit. Although the argument as expressed here is put in rather more precise mathematical form than usual, it would not be unfair to say that broadly speaking those on the left in politics are inclined to argue that gains to total benefit by more even income distribution more than offset the consequential losses via R and I — if these really exist — while those on the right would argue the reverse. At least at this stage it is not the intention that this analysis should get involved with political disagreements so that comments on this controversy will be fairly muted except to say first that there is very little evidence, on the basis of international comparison, that different tax systems have the slightest measurable impact on economic performance, and second that over the broad mass of tax payers there is not much evidence that any tax systems involve much redistribution at all, net of all collection and disbursements, except roughly from the top 5%

of income earners to the bottom 20%. For the remaining 75% the net effect of the tax system is more or less neutral. Nor is there any substantial evidence that consumption distributions tend to alter appreciably with faster or slower rates of economic growth, or that they have altered very much over quite long time spans. The stability of the distribution of income post tax and social security in the U.K. has already been cited. Of course this is a separate question from the proportion of the national income which is consumed; this is well above the international average in Britain.[29] Inevitably with a higher growth rate the proportion of the national income which was consumed would have to fall while the proportion devoted to investment rose. This would involve higher retained profits for enterprises and more saving by individuals or by the government, but not necessarily any change in the distribution of consumption. The rather depressing conclusion we must therefore arrive at is that although there appears to be a strong *prima facie* case for increasing benefit by a process of reducing the distribution of income, at least after tax, the political and practical difficulties involved in doing so are such that the prospects for any major gains from this quarter do not look very promising, however important those on the left in politics may think such gains are. Regrettable though it may be, it seems to be the case that it is much more likely that agreement will be obtained on courses of action to increase the benefit gained from the economy by increasing the size of the cake rather than by dividing it up more equally.

Turning now to wealth distribution the main problem to be faced in Britain is that there is no doubt that an accelerating rate of growth, if it could be achieved, would make the wealthy even richer, and furthermore there is good reason to believe that the rate at which this process occurs would be far greater than the rate at which the national incomes would rise. The explanation for this is that a rapid increase in economic growth in the U.K. would certainly entail a substantial increase in the profitability of the commercial and industrial sectors, and this combined with far better prospects for the future would inevitably lead to a very marked stock exchange boom. While it is true that the distribution of wealth in the United Kingdom has lessened over the last seven years the main reason why this has happened is because the market for equity shares has gone up very little in money terms while the prices for everything else have risen steadily. Lack of economic growth, and hence dreary prospects for company earnings have been responsible. However, once a substantial movement to more rapid growth established itself this process would be reversed. It may be that there would be some offsetting factors to this worsening distribution of wealth in time, such as more owner occupation of housing, a tendency which has been very marked in the United States, but nevertheless the immediate results of more rapid economic growth would undoubtedly be a more uneven distribution of wealth. To avoid the social strains involved in this process becoming intolerable it would almost certainly be necessary to do something about the very feeble wealth taxes which exist in the U.K. at present. It is an unpleasant fact that although the U.K. has got one of the most equitable post tax distributions of income in the world, our distribution of wealth is about the least equitable anywhere outside the Middle East. The ways in which wealth could be taxed without the side effects being very damaging have been widely canvassed, some form of gift tax being the favourable candidate, and it should be recognised that a strongly enforced tax of this type on the very wealthy may well be a minimum *quid pro quo* for the special advantage they would receive from higher rates of growth.

However, this line of analysis is not directly related to total benefit which is more concerned with income flows than capital appreciation, or, more precisely is only concerned with capital appreciation in so far as it leads to claims on current resources. The only way in which this can happen is for people to spend capital rather than income, in other words to dis-save. Total benefit would be affected if it were to be supposed that this process would be more likely to happen at one rate of growth rather than another, but it is difficult to see any reason why this should happen. In general therefore it seems that wealth distribution is not a factor which is likely to have much effect on total benefit except in so far as mitigation of worsening distribution of wealth may be a necessary policy desideratum to avoid social strains which might themselves upset the right environment for growth.

Part 4   Conclusion

Welfare Analysis – Summary of Results

We are now in a position to summarise the results which have been achieved so far. With certain assumptions about factors D and d we have derived expressions for getting the best out of the economy in terms of two main variables — I, the proportion of the national income, or net national product, which is reinvested, and R which is specifically a measure of the return on investment which is being obtained, and in which in a more general sense is a measure of the overall efficiency with which the economy is being run year by year. The expression relating these variables together can be used to derive optimum policies for economic growth, in particular showing what proportion of the national income should be reinvested to best advantage in relation to the return on investment that can be achieved. It has also been possible to relax all the restrictions put upon the model when it was first being constructed without it getting unduly complicated, or unrealistic, or without any of the main assumptions upon which it was built becoming weakened. Furthermore it has been possible to relate all the other policy goals which are considered desirable to the one main maximand with the very great advantage that it is now possible to put them into at least some sort of weighted rank order. We have also had an opportunity to see what secondary effects we must look for and allow for, so that even if some of the policy objectives turn out not to be very important in themselves we can make provision for their side effects which may be significant.

Taking all the main policy objectives in turn it has been found that getting the right conditions for economic growth has a far larger effect on total benefit than any other factor — or, indeed, all the rest put together. However it has emerged that values for total benefit are not only dependent on the right amount of investment of the national income being carried out, but they are even more dependent on a high return from investment being achieved. In other words obtaining high values for R is even more important than getting the right value for I. Although more detailed analysis of the conditions for high values for R will follow in the next chapter, it has been strongly hinted already that a high and rising level of demand has a great deal to do with high values of R and it is therefore particularly important that the weight to be attached to any policy objective which is likely to conflict with these conditions should be looked at very carefully.

It has been found that there is little gain in total benefit to be found from balance of payments policy, the best goal here being to ensure that, taking one year with another, a balance is maintained without surpluses or deficits. Exchange rate policy, on the other hand, has more potential for leading (though not directly) to improved values of total benefit, although we found that total benefit would be adversely affected by devaluation to the extent of the percentage change in the terms of trade times the proportion of the national income involved with overseas trade. We also found, contrary to popular beliefs, that devaluation was not likely to have a marked effect on the terms of trade. However, devaluation may lead indirectly to a much better environment for high values of I and R, although there may be a risk of worse inflation if the rise in domestic prices caused by devaluation is not absorbed by higher output quickly enough. Quantitative analysis of this point must wait until the next chapter. Nonetheless, overall the possibilities for affecting total benefit directly by balance of payments or exchange rate policy appear to be very small, and therefore they should be treated as restraints or policy weapons rather than as objectives.

Our investigations of the arguments against inflation produced very little of any substance to show that inflation of itself up to levels of 10% or so p.a. and perhaps even higher need have any effect whatever on the benefit received from economic output. However there were two ways in which inflation could have an adverse influence, one being via the balance of payments and the other by misallocation of resources. The balance of payments problem can be circumvented by a more flexible exchange rate policy, and the problem over misallocation of resources, while difficult to quantify exactly, did not appear to be very substantial, at least over the comparatively low levels of inflation which are likely to be experienced in the U.K. Since the misallocation of resources problem is the only one of any strength which emerged from all the alleged demerits of inflation, stability of prices as an objective turns out to be surprisingly insubstantial and one which we can afford to ignore provided it is quite clear that the risk to R from misallocation of resources is more than offset by clear gains in other directions which may risk inflation as a consequence.

Full employment − of capital resources as well as people − as a policy emerges as one which entails clear gains that are approximately of the order of twice the reduction of the registered unemployed as a percentage of those in employment. While there are dangers of inflation and bottlenecks if this policy is pushed too far, there seems no reason why either the inflationary consequences or the bottleneck problems should become so acute as to offset the gains to total benefit from fuller employment until unemployment has fallen to the levels consistently maintained in other countries of 1% or even less.

Finally, as regards income and wealth distribution it was found that, while there is definitely scope for improving total benefit via a more equitable distribution of income, this objective was one which was so involved with conflicts of interest as to be more in the domain of politics than economics. This is particularly so because there is at least some scope for disagreement about both the practicality of income redistribution and the side effects on R and I. Certainly there is no reason to believe that consumption distribution, especially net of tax, is likely to become more uneven with higher rates of growth. The same cannot be said, however, of wealth distribution which is bound to worsen with high growth rates making some sort of offsetting wealth tax desirable to preserve a reasonable social balance. The effects of worsening wealth distribution on the current flow of resources, with which total benefit is concerned, were found to be negligible.

Welfare Analysis — Defence and Appraisal

This is as far as the theoretical analysis in this book can take us before we move on to the section devoted to using the results from the model which has been developed to evolve a new economic policy for the U.K., which puts the conclusion we have reached into practice. However, before doing so it would be in order first to consider ways in which the model development process used can be attacked so that the limitations of what has been achieved can be clearly seen, and second to stand back and try and assess what positive achievements can be claimed.

There are several different lines of attack in fact. The first is what one might call the plain man's approach. Is it really possible to derive economic policies from such ethereal considerations as the extent to which people discount the future and the rate at which the marginal utility of income falls? Is not welfare economics too vague and insubstantial a subject to stand the weight of analysis which the model developed in this chapter imposes upon it? The answer to this line of attack is straight-forward. It is quite impossible to come to any opinion at all about economic growth or, indeed, most other aspects of economic management unless one does have some views about such subjects as discounting the future and the importance or value of extra income, and in fact when pressed it is found that all plain men do have views on these subjects although they are perhaps rather confused or undeveloped. All that has been done in the process of model development here is to make the underlying assumptions completely explicit. More than that, the margins of error involved in these assumptions have been very carefully investigated at all stages so that the consequences of the assumptions made being wrong can be assessed too. Furthermore at all stages we have been at pains to avoid any assumptions which conflict with common sense. If the plain man's attack amounted to a charge that mathematical analysis was being applied to an area which defied quantification it would be justified, but the submission made here is that this is not the case. The subject we are concerned with is amenable to mathematical treatment provided the assumptions made are chosen carefully, and to eschew the advantages of quantification in these circumstances would be to take a very reactionary step. The plain man's attack is on systematic treatment, not on the assumptions made, which he might well share himself if he thought about them.

The next line of attack is that too many assumptions are made for the policy recommendations which emerge at the end to have any serious weight. This might be a serious line to criticism but for one remarkable quality which the model developed shows at every stage, and this might be called, for want of a better term, convergence. Investigation of each assumption made, particularly those to do with factors D and d (which are the most insubstantial and therefore the most difficult to deal with) shows that a wide margin of error can be allowed in the shape of these assumptions before any serious difference is made to the policy recommendations, or to the relative measurements of results of the different policies which emerge. Also, in every case a variation in assumption made about the size of either D or d leads to a much smaller proportional variation in either prescription or relative measurement in the expressions which have been developed. If the reverse were true, and the prescriptions and measurements were very unstable, in that they were very sensitive to changes in the assumptions upon which the model was built, then the value of the whole approach adopted could much more be called easily into question. But this quality of convergence is the best safeguard against this line of attack which could be had, and the fact that it is so marked is cause for particular confidence that even if some of the assumptions made are not quite right the broad conclusion arrived at can still be relied on. This is particularly so in view of the enormous importance which the model shows should be attached to achieving the right growth environment as against other objectives. Even if the difference were much narrower, the model could still be relied on to discriminate between one objective and another, but in view of the wide disparity in importance thrown up between economic growth and all the other desiderata combined with the model's convergent quality, the assumptions made would have to be unbelievably wrong before the main conclusions failed to follow.

A somewhat different version of the same line of objection is to attack the basis on which our assumptions about d were made by calling in question the relationship between prices, costs and value. Of course this is a fundamental attack on the capacity of economics generally to be taken as a serious object of study, and not just on the model developed here. For this reason in particular it deserves an answer. The line of argument is as follows: on the supply side there is considerable evidence that some goods and services are charged at much higher prices than others in relation to their long run cost, for example it has been suggested already on page 61 that the entire output of the public sector in the U.K. is undercharged for by some 5% - 10% compared to the private sector — a phenomenon which has got nothing to do with supply and demand. What are prices supposed to reflect in these circumstances? There are also more fundamental reasons for grave suspicion about prices. It is a remarkable fact that at least the anticipated return on capital employed is the same whether old or new goods and services are being produced. Is this because wants have appeared for new goods and services which can just be sold at prices that keep the return on capital employed constant, or is it not in fact far more likely that prices have simply been administered to cover all long run production costs including profit and rent? And if this is true, why should the benefit from the latest set of inventions be the same as those of earlier ones, even if as a matter of coincidence they happen to cost the same? Even if prices did accurately reflect costs on the supply side there is still the problem of whether benefit can reasonably be related to prices. Clearly some expenditure gives more pleasure than others — an orangeade gives more pleasure to a thirsty man than a bottle of champagne to one who has had enough already. If we are dealing with the benefit which people receive from economic output are we not faced with the classical surplus value problem? If prices reflect accurately neither costs nor benefit how can we use financial units at all as a basis for economic prescription? And finally, what about economic benefits which are not charged for at all such as leisure and the labour of the housewife?

There are several different problems here. With regard to systematic undercharging of the type to be found in the U.K. public sector there are financial restraints which will stop the bias from this factor being too serious, and in any case if the bias continues from year to year to the same extent then the effects on our analysis of factor d can be ignored completely because the bias will be systematic. The surplus value problem can be disposed of in a similar way. Marginal analysis superseded surplus value analysis largely because it was realised that marginal analysis concentrated on the really important area where a balance was being struck between supply and demand. The fact that this point was measured by a price related marginal analysis firmly to the real world and the problems of surplus value could then be assumed to be, on average, the same for every product, so that, even if prices did not measure what we have called benefit exactly, they were in some way proportional to it − and that is all that is needed to get over this problem, at least in a static situation. Of course, in our analysis here we are not positing that benefit is directly proportional to prices because we have introduced a number of factors to explain systematically why this should not be so. However, it still remains very important that the prices to which our analysis relates should be meaningful, otherwise the whole structure collapses. Thus even if we can dispose of the surplus value problem in the same way as is done with marginal analysis, we are still faced with the problem of technical advance leading to administered prices for new products. However, here too marginal analysis can rescue us fairly easily. While the mix of output from the economy evidently alters from year to year, and so do the relative prices of many of the products and services of which the output is comprised, a rough balance at least is maintained between the relative supply of and demand for all the goods and services turned out by the economy via the reigning price structure, with old products and services competing with new ones on the same market. If our analysis of d is going to be upset, it would have to be shown that there was a non-systematic bias appearing over time with surplus value either rising or falling by a substantial amount for the economy's product mix − not for income as a whole, which, of course, has already been allowed for in our assumption of a falling marginal utility of income. It seems difficult to believe that surplus value is changing in this fashion, and the safest assumption to make seems to be that it is not altering at all. However, even if it were, it is not clear that our assumptions about d would be upset very much, and it has already been proved that the model we have developed can have a substantial error in our assumptions about d before the conclusions from it are materially altered.

This leaves us with the problem of economic benefits which are not charged for in national accounts such as leisure, the output of the housewife, and other similar problems which are buried in the accounting conventions used in compiling national accounts. Again the answer to these problems is partly that they do not upset our analysis provided any bias they introduce is systematic (i.e. roughly the same every year), and partly that efforts to rewrite national accounts using different ratios seldom make very much difference to the final outcome. We have seen this already ourselves on pages 36-37, and others who have used other conventions have come to much the same broad conclusion.[30] We therefore arrive at the conclusion that our analysis is no more vulnerable than economics as a whole to undermining by attack on the premises from which it is built up, and in particular the application of Occam's razor to the relationship between prices and benefit in the form of marginal analysis of prices enables us to ground our welfare analysis firmly in units which can be related back to the real world.

A third general line of attack on the model developed in this chapter is more a matter of temperament — that the approach adopted is too rational and too optimistic, and that the results hoped for will never be achieved. Are we in fact going to be able to increase our rate of growth by investing more, or is the investment going to go to waste in deflation forced upon us by intransigent circumstances beyond our control? And even if it is possible to increase the rate of growth of the economy by investing more and by running our affairs more efficiently, this involves some extra sacrifice of benefit today to achieve more tomorrow. Furthermore this is a sacrifice which has got to be made by society as a whole, and where the increasing benefit will be spread over everyone, including all those who dodge the column and avoid doing any sacrificing themselves. In these circumstances is not everyone going to try and get someone else to do the extra sacrificing so that in the end none or very little is done? And even supposing these problems could be overcome so that the national income does start rising more rapidly, there are offsetting factors in the form of extra pollution, increasing congestion, despoliation and exhaustion of natural resources, which may turn the increase in incomes to ashes. Let it be said straightaway that these are very real dangers, and not ones which can be easily explained away. However, like the economic problems this book is mainly concerned with, these political and social problems are not insuperable, and increasing the national income can make more resources available to fight pollution, despoliation, congestion and exhaustion of natural resources as well as making these problems worse. Similarly the strain on the political system involved in increasing the efficiency with which our economy is run is very much a function of the intelligence and subtlety with which policies to achieve this end are put into practice. It is up to the reader to decide whether the policies proposed in the next chapter are practical or not. The objections of the pessimist do not undermine the analysis presented above; but they do reinforce the point that economic analysis by itself does not solve political and social problems.

Finally, it can be argued that the analysis throughout this chapter is open to the gravest philosophical objections on the grounds that it is one long naturalistic fallacy, arguing continuously from what is to what ought to be done. This is particularly the case in all the discussion about the extent to which we should allow for the amount by which people discount the future. Indeed at one point it was argued that ethical restraints ought to be put upon the extent to which people should be allowed to discount the future. However, this point is easily answered. The model built up in this chapter is no more or less solidly utilitarian than almost all others in the social sciences, and as such it is concerned quite properly with considering what people want and then explaining how their desires can be attained. If some people are more short sighted than the average there is no reason why their attitudes should be allowed to jeopardise the policies adopted for the economy as a whole if it can be clearly shown that the general welfare would suffer as a result. However, the limits of a utilitarian approach should be recognised, and in particular it should be noted that utilitarianism can lead to conflicts with political attitudes which are drawn from other political philosophies.

Having examined the various ways in which the model developed in this chapter can be objected to it is now time to turn to what can be claimed for it.

In the first place a theory has been developed which not only shows how important economic growth is as an objective, but shows this in a quantitative manner, related to all the other policy goals which have been put forward. Furthermore, the analysis already carried out hints strongly what steps should be taken to improve the performance of the economy, and in the next chapter this prescription will be developed in much more detail to show how the theory could be put into practice. In addition, a measure of the overall results being achieved from any economy — total benefit — has been produced, which is a far more sophisticated measuring rod than any available at the moment. It does not simply award high marks to any economy which is growing quickly, but provides a measure of all the major factors to be considered, including the sacrifice involved in faster growth. A high value for total benefit implies that a rational use is being made of all the economic resources available, and a low one means the opposite. Despite the importance of economic growth as an objective, other factors are given their due weight so that the correlation between total benefit for different countries and their rates of growth is not one to one. This is a big step forward from the usual league tables, not only in that the rank order may be different, but also because the difference in efficiency or rationality in the way different economies are being run can be measured and quantified. The value of total benefit for this or any other economy is not very meaningful by itself, but its value in relation to the value for other economies is a direct measure of the extent to which the economy is being run in an efficient and rational manner.

These results have been achieved by analysis which is neither unduly complex or restricted by unrealistic assumptions. It is firmly related to the real world and therefore it is easy to see how its results can be applied to real world situations as we shall see in the next chapter. If other objectives than those considered here are to be included as policy goals, such as what the implications would be of Britain joining the Common Market, then the model is flexible enough to incorporate these without any weakening of its assumptions or its prescriptive value. Finally the significance of all the assumptions made during the model building process has been carefully investigated at all stages, and the strong convergent quality which we have found lends support to the view that the prescriptions which emerge can be relied upon to be right within narrow limits. It is also perhaps worth pointing out that the analysis presented here also completely bypasses the problems current growth economics becomes involved with in trying to approach dynamic economics from premises which are essentially related to static situations. This has been achieved by working in non-financial units, which can however be related back to the real world. A final submission is that this points the way ahead for a much more productive approach to the problems involved with growth economics than much of the methodology currently in vogue.

Where the analysis presented so far is somewhat deficient is in showing what the optimum path from the present to the preferred policy mix should be. This is a line of theory development which could follow on from the model already developed. What would be required would be to establish with more accuracy than has been possible during the preparation of this book the values of such variables as what the trade-offs between inflation and reductions in the value of R actually are for different levels of inflation, and where the point actually is where the gains from less unemployment are offset by the losses via other factors. Once these, and a number of other relationships had been established with as much accuracy as possible, various restraints would have to be introduced such as the maximum rate at which investment could be expanded, the minimum current increases in standard of living which people are prepared to accept, etc., and it would then be possible to produce a series of equations defining the optimum path for the economy to take in the future. In fact, in the next chapter, the fruits of a considerable amount of research on these variables and restraints will be presented so that a policy prescription can be produced for Britain for the next five years. However, the development of this policy is *ad hoc*, and it would be very worthwhile if a more general theory in this area could be developed, including, if possible, removal of the one restraint which was not dealt with in this book, *viz* the question of subsistence levels. That would round the picture off to give a truly general optimum economic policy theory.

Chapter III A New Policy— Prescriptions for the British Economy

Part 1 Introduction

The objective in this chapter is to apply the prescriptions from the model developed in Chapter II to the British economy. The starting point is to investigate what has happened in the U.K. and elsewhere over the last few years so that we can see why our performance has been so poor, and what lessons there are to be learnt from the experience of other countries. Armed with the analytical weapons from the last chapter we then move on to constructing a five year budget showing what could be done to achieve a transformation in our economic circumstances. This is followed by an investigation into the methods currently employed by the authorities in this country for deciding what types of investment should be carried out, the conclusion being that a very substantial change of emphasis is required. We then turn to the effects of our joining the Common Market on our economic prospects and construct another budget showing what is likely to happen in Britain over the next five years if present policies continue. Finally a general appraisal is made of the possible weaknesses in all the policies proposed, so that the margins of error within which we are working are estimated as carefully as possible, and then the advantages of the new proposals are evaluated in comparison to what is likely to happen if present policies continue.

The British Economy — 1950 - 1970

In Table III.1 there will be found set out the record of what has been achieved by the British economy over the period 1950-1970. Since tables such as these are the basis for most of the prescription to be

Table III.1

Summary of the Performance of the British Economy 1949-70

1	2	3	4	5	6	7	8
Year	GDP FC	Capital Con-sumption	NDP FC	GDCF	Increase St & WIP	5 + 6 Gross Invest-ment	7 – 3 Net Invest-ment
1949	18,297	1,395	16,902	2,497	87	2,584	1,189
1950	18,889	1,446	17,443	2,632	(265)	2,367	921
1951	19,564	1,493	18,071	2,642	593	3,235	1,742
1952	19,557	1,530	18,027	2,653	63	2,716	1,186
1953	20,469	1,586	18,883	2,941	130	3,071	1,485
1954	21,206	1,653	19,553	3,191	52	3,243	1,590
1955	21,930	1,724	20,206	3,371	302	3,673	1,949
1956	22,343	1,775	20,568	3,525	235	3,760	1,985
1957	22,773	1,838	20,935	3,712	241	3,953	2,115
1958	22,706	1,903	20,803	3,737	107	3,844	1,941
1959	23,491	1,974	21,517	4,025	188	4,213	2,239
1960	24,639	2,058	22,581	4,418	628	5,046	2,988
Ten Year Totals	18,317			34,926	1,733	36,659	18,342
1961	25,527	2,144	23,373	4,847	327	5,174	3,030
1962	25,780	2,222	23,558	4,829	66	4,895	2,673
1963	26,793	2,318	24,475	4,912	191	5,103	2,785
1964	28,259	2,434	25,825	5,725	628	6,353	3,919
1965	29,030	2,546	26,484	5,960	376	6,336	3,790
1966	29,640	2,664	26,976	6,112	254	6,366	3,702
1967	30,182	2,805	27,377	6,524	184	6,708	3,903
1968	31,127	2,939	28,188	6,850	158	7,008	4,069
1969	31,655	3,073	28,582	6,777	346	7,123	4,050
1970	32,182	3,213	28,969	6,886	329	7,215	4,002
Ten Year Totals	25,203			56,954	3,158	60,112	34,909

Source: 1971 *National Income and Expenditure Blue Book* supplemented by *Annual Abstract of Statistics* published by H.M.S.O. All financial figures at 1963 prices.

found in this chapter, it would be in order to explain in some detail how these tables have been made up.

The first thing to be noted is that all the figures presented have been adjusted to allow for the effects of inflation, and along the lines of standard current OECD practice the base year chosen is 1963 — the

9	10	11	12	13	14	15	16
Year on Year Increase NDP FC	Crude R	Total Working Pop. in Employment (1000)	Annual Increase	% Annual Increase	Actual R	N.N.P. F.C.	8 as Ratio 15 I
		23,069				17,219	.0690
541	.4550	23,236	167	.72	.3782	17,957	.0512
628	.6818	23,576	340	1.46	.4754	18,404	.0946
(44)	(.0252)	23,527	(49)	(.21)	(.0096)	18,271	.0649
856	.7217	23,641	114	.48	.6670	19,128	.0776
670	.4511	23,993	352	1.49	.3100	19,822	.0802
653	.4106	24,286	293	1.22	.2987	20,379	.0956
362	.1857	24,464	178	.73	.1297	20,799	.0954
367	.1848	24,497	33	.13	.1755	21,178	.0998
(132)	(.0624)	24,227	(270)	(1.10)	.0187	21,107	.0919
714	.3678	24,300	73	.30	.3442	21,789	.1027
1064	.4752	24,774	474	1.95	.3349	:22,819:	.1309
5679	.3096		1705	7.39	.2585	216,053	.0848
792	.2650	25,057	283	1.14	.2008	23,632	.1282
185	.0610	25,214	157	.63	.0248	23,900	.1118
917	.3430	25,222	8	.03	.3412	24,873	.1119
1350	.4847	25,200	278	1.10	.4126	26,196	.1496
659	.1681	25,750	250	.98	.1200	26,901	.1408
492	.1298	25,894	144	.56	.1004	27,349	.1353
401	.1083	25,483	(411)	(1.59)	.1950	27,737	.1407
811	.2077	25,283	(200)	(.78)	.2484	28,475	.1428
394	.0968	25,284	1	—	.0968	28,995	.1396
387	.0955	25,080	(202)	(.81)	.1378	:29,365:	.1362
6388	.1829		308	1.24	.1769	260,877	.1338

First Period   D   D   Second Period D   D
ΣB = .90 10.96   .93 16.88 ΣB= .90 10.51   .93 16.27
          .91 12.42   .94 20.49   .91 11.93   .94 19.79
          .92 14.32   .95 25.93   .92 13.77   .95 25.11
Average = 16.83   Average 16.23

same as in the National Income Blue Book. It will also be noted that all the values are at factor cost and not at market prices for the reasons explained on page 38. Turning now to individual columns, column 2 shows the Gross *Domestic* Product because we are concerned with the effects of investment within the domestic economy, where the full social return comes back to the domestic residents, rather than with investment abroad, and this is why column 5 is also a measure of domestic investment. The figures in column 3 are a not wholly satisfactory measure of what has to be taken away from Gross Investment (column 7) to produce Net Investment (column 8), but no other figures are readily available, especially on a comparable international basis. Therefore, with all the reservations already explained in the last chapter, they will have to be taken as the nearest available approximation to what we are looking for. Taking Capital Consumption from Gross Domestic Product provides the figures in column 3 for Net Domestic Product. Column 6 measures Increases in Stocks and Work in Progress, and insofar as these increases are an absolutely unavoidable concomitant of other forms of investment they have been added to the figures in column 5 to produce the figures for Gross Investment in column 7. Column 3 has then been subtracted from column 7 to produce values for Net Investment. Column 9 shows the year on year increase in Net Domestic Product and is obtained from the annual differences in column 4. The figures shown in brackets are negative, because instead of there being increases in some years there were actually decreases in the Net Domestic Product.

Column 10 is a crude measure of R, not allowing for any changes in the labour force, and is the ratio obtained by taking the increase in Net Domestic Product for any given year and dividing it by the figure in column 8 for the previous year. Column 11 shows the Total Working Population in Employment, and thus excludes the unemployed. Column 12 shows the annual increase or decrease (in brackets) and column 13 the same as a percentage. Column 14 is the value for R obtained by making the following adjustments. It is assumed that a 1% change in the labour force would make a ¾% change in Net Domestic Product with no alteration at all to the amount of capital employed, since this is approximately the ratio of the factor rewards on average throughout the economy; an increase in those in employment of say 1% this year as compared to last year is thus assumed to be responsible for ¾% increase in the Net Domestic Product this year compared with last year, irrespective of what the investment situation is. Net investment the previous year is assumed to account for the residual and column 14 is therefore a measure of the social return actually being obtained from investment after allowing for changes in the size of the labour force.

It may seem unreasonable to assume that large or small increases in the Net Domestic Product should be attributed so solidly to changes in the return on investment rather than to changes in labour productivity of those still in employment, but the answer to this criticism is that these are but the two sides of the same coin. What we are concerned with in this measurement of R is not what the potential return on investment would be if the right conditions obtained — which of course would involve achieving all the potential gains in labour productivity from all the investment which had been made — but what results have actually been achieved. All we are concerned with doing at this stage is to try and separate out three different factors, all of which could be measured in terms of labour. One is to find out what increases in output could be obtained by improving the productivity of those in employment, of which R is the appropriate measure, the second is to find out what increases could be gained from fuller employment, so that more people are involved in the productive process; and the third is to find out what the effects on the economy would be of an overall increase in the labour force due to growth in the population of working age, or more willingness to participate in employment. The procedure adopted is the simplest way of isolating the effects of these three factors.

Column 15, the Net National Product is obtained by adding to column 4 Net Property Income from Abroad, which has been excluded thus far on the grounds that it had nothing to do with the returns on domestic investment, though there seems to be no good reason for excluding this income from being available for investment. Net National Product is the same as the National Income. Finally in column 16 we have a measure of I, taken as being the figures in column 8 as a ratio of those in column 15.

Before discussing the actual figures there is one last explanation to be made about the way the tables are laid out. As well as showing the picture year by year they also demonstrate what was happening in the two ten year periods which made up the twenty years, and so not only are the average results obtained over a long enough period of time for the worst fluctuations to be ironed out, but they also show the overall trend of events between one decade and the next. To obtain ten year figures it is necessary to ensure that the ten years of investment are taken one year further back than the ten years of resulting output, because of the average one year time lag posited, and this explains, for example, why the total for Net Investment for the first decade is actually the total for 1949-1959, whereas the increased output to which this is related occurred in the years 1950-1960. Average values of R and I for these ten year periods have also been calculated so that an overall measure of the efficiency with which the economy was being run can be calculated not just for individual years but for the two decades as well.

Turning now to the actual values of R and I thrown up in Table III.1, the first thing to note is the very wide spread of values appearing for R. The spread of values for R was greater in the earlier decade, varying in value from $-.0096$ to $.6670$, but it was still very large in the second decade, varying from $.0968$ to $.4126$. It is also very depressing to note that the average value for R fell heavily from the first decade to the second, from $.2585$ to $.1769$. Based on the analysis in the last chapter the procedure for calculating total benefit used here is to take the unweighted average of all the values of ΣB, in terms of I and R, with values of D from $.90$ to $.95$, and then adjust the figure obtained as follows:

Unemployment: the value for total benefit should be reduced by twice the percentage of the potential working population which was unemployed, which was 1.3%[1] on average in the 50's and 1.6%[1] during the 60's.

Inflation: since we found no evidence that inflation reduced the benefit which people received from any given level of output, no adjustment to total benefit needs to be made on this score; any reduction in output caused by inflation, via misallocation of resources, balance of payments troubles, etc. is already accounted for in the value for R.

Foreign Exchange: we have seen in earlier sections of this book that alterations in the external value of the domestic currency do not usually alter the terms of trade at all appreciably. Over the period of the 1967 devaluation import and export prices rose by almost exactly the same amount[2] so that the terms of trade remained as they were. During the 1960's there was no appreciable alteration in the terms of trade at all so that no change in the vlue of total benefit needs to be made for this period on this account.[3] However, during the 1950's there was a very marked improvement in our terms of trade — which was nothing to do with any devalutation — of the order of 27%.[4] The adjustment to be made to total benefit is to multiply the change in the terms of trade by the proportion of the national income devoted to foreign trade, which also happened to be 27%[5] during the period. However, the improvement in the terms of trade did not all take place at the beginning of the decade: about half came early on after the end of the Korean War, and half at the end. Over the period the *average* improvement in the terms of trade was about 13.5%. This is quite a substantial adjustment. The other adjustment which might have to be made related to the accumulation of large reserves on current account; however this was not a noticeable feature of either the 50's or the 60's.

Calculation of values for total benefit for the U.K. for the 1950's and 60's is therefore completed as follows:

D	1950's	1960's
.90	10.96	10.51
.91	12.42	11.93
.92	14.32	13.77
.93	16.88	16.27
.94	20.49	19.79
.95	<u>25.93</u>	<u>25.11</u>

	1950's	1960's
Unweighted Average for Total Benefit	16.83	16.23
Unemployment adjustment	(2.6%)	(3.2%)
Terms of Trade adjustment	3.6%	—
Final Total Benefit	16.98	15.71

It will be noted that these figures show a fall in total benefit of 8% between the 50's and 60's. Even if the improvement in the terms of trade is excluded, there was still a fall of just over 4%. This very poor result was achieved despite a very substantial increase in the proportion of the national income devoted to net investment, which rose from 8.9% in the '50's to 13.4% in the '60's. Clearly raising I on its own is no solution to raising total benefit if R simply falls *pro rata*. It is now time to turn, therefore, to analysing the relationship between R and I, and to considering in evidence both details of the performance of the British economy and also what has been achieved elsewhere in the world.

Part 2   New Policy Parameters

The Relationship between the Savings/Investment Ratio and the Social Rate of Return

It was seen in the last chapter that higher values of total benefit could be obtained partly by reducing unemployment, improving the terms of trade if this is possible, etc., but there is no doubt that by far the greatest gains were to be made by raising R and I together, particularly if higher values of I were associated with higher values for R. In other words the greater the value for R the more worthwhile higher values of I become. It is therefore extremely material to try to discover what tends to produce one value of R rather than another, and to establish whether there is likely to be any systematic relationship between R and I.

As regards the relationship between R and I there are widely varying views. Some commentators have inclined to the opinion that the amount of investment which it is worth undertaking is determined by the growth of the labour force and by technical progress, so that increasing I simply reduces R by the same proportion.[6] Others have been inclined to take the view that the relationship between I and R is not likely to alter as more investment is undertaken; while a still more optimistic school of thought thinks it likely that as I rises so should R, because with higher values of I one gets a larger proportion of manufacturing as against social investment, and the former has a higher social rate of return than the latter.[7]

The contention in this book is that any one of these three views may be correct, and there is evidence of all three relationships to be found in Table III.1. However, which of the three relationships obtain in any given circumstances is not a matter of chance, but a combination of two elements both of which are amenable to control by policy. One is the type of investment which is undertaken, and the second is the extent to which it is utilised once it is installed. We shall be considering what sort of investment should make the greatest contribution to growth later; we must now consider the evidence that the value of R obtained in any circumstances is largely determined not so much by any intrinsic quality of the pattern of investment undertaken as by the intensiveness of the use which is made of it.

Even a cursory examination of Table III.1 points strongly in this direction. By no stretch of the imagination could the changes in the values of R thrown up be attributed solely to changes in the intrinsic capacity of the investment being made to produce extra output between one year and another. It is utterly inconceivable that the investment undertaken in 1961 should have a potential social rate of return of .0248 while that undertaken in 1962 and one of .3412. Still less could one conceive that the investment undertaken in 1951 had a negative capacity for producing extra output while the 1952 investment produced a social rate of return of .6670. Let it be repeated that the explanation of these wide variations lies, of course, to some extent in the intrinsic potential of the investment made, but that by far the largest element causing these swings in the value of R had nothing to do with the potential of the investment made at all. What it did depend on was the extent to which the investment made was being used. What really makes more difference to the value of R than anything else — and as we shall see this is true in the longer term as well as the short term — is the pressure of demand in the economy. High pressure of demand produces high values of R, and low pressure of demand, or deflation, produces low values. For those not too familiar with the details of recent British economic history the following fairly detailed table shows the position all too clearly, particularly when it is borne in mind that there is a time lag of a few months between the announcement of policy changes and the effects they have on the state of the economy:

Table III.2[8]

Year	R	I		Principal Changes in Policy
1951	.4754	.0946	Jan:	£4,700m rearmament programme announced.
			Apr:	Gaitskell's budget; tax increases and Health Service charges.
1952	(.0096)	.0649	Jan:	Import restrictions, capital investment cuts, H.P. restrictions
			Mar:	Neutral budget.
1953	.6670	.0776	Apr:	Budget 6d off income tax.
1954	.3100	.0802	Apr:	Neutral budget; new investment allowances.
1955	.2987	.0956	Feb:	Moderate H.P controls reintroduced.
			Apr:	Budget 6d off income tax etc.

Table III.2 (continued)

Year	R	I	Principal Changes in Policy	
1955 (continued)			Jul:	Further H.P. restrictions; squeeze on bank advances; capital investment cuts by nationalised industries.
			Oct:	Autumn budget; purchase tax increases etc.
1956	.1297	.0954	Feb:	More H.P. controls; investment allowances suspended; cuts in public investment.
			Apr:	Neutral budget.
1957	.1755	.0998	Apr:	Budget; surtax concessions.
			Sept:	Bank Rate raised to 7%; ceiling on public sector spending and bank advances.
1958	.0187	.0919	Apr:	Budget; small purchase tax reliefs
			Jul-Oct:	Gradual relaxation of credit controls and public expenditure limits.
1959	.3442	.1027	Apr:	Tax relief budget.
1960	.3349	.1309	Apr:	Neutral budget but later in month H.P. restrictions reintroduced, credit squeeze.
1961	.2008	.1282	Jan:	H.P. restrictions ceased.
			Apr:	Budget; surtax relief, profits tax increase, fuel oil tax.
			Jul:	Crisis measures; Bank Rate raised to 7%; regulator; government expenditure checked; credit squeeze.
1962	.0248	.1118	Apr:	Budget; short term capital gains tax and other minor changes.
			June:	Small H.P. tax relaxations.
			Nov:	Increased investment allowances etc; purchase tax on cars reduced.
1963	.3412	.1119	Apr:	Budget; reliefs for families and depressed regions.
1964	.4126	.1496	Apr:	£100m of increased taxation on drink and tobacco.
			Oct:	Measures to reduce balance of payments deficit.
			Nov:	Direct and indirect taxation increased; pensions increased.
1965	.1200	.1408	Apr:	Budget; tax increased by over £200m.
			Jun:	Bank Rate cut; H.P. restrictions eased.
			Jul:	Cuts in government investment, tighter exchange controls, H.P. restrictions.
1966	.1004	.1353	Feb:	Tighter H.P. restrictions.
			May:	Budget neutral.
			Jul:	Crisis measures; regulator increase, government spending curb, H.P. controls tightened.

Table III.2 (continued)

Year	R	I	Principal Changes in Policy		
1967	.1950	.1407	Apr:	Neutral budget.	
			Jun:	H.P. relaxations.	
			Aug:	Further H.P. relaxations	
			Nov:	Devaluation of sterling from $2.80 to $2.40.	
1968	.2484	.1428	Jan:	Public expenditure curbs announced.	
			Mar:	Budget; tax increases totalling £923m; purchase tax increases. S.E.T. up by 50% etc.	
			Nov:	H.P. restrictions tightened.	
1969	.0968	.1396	Apr:	Budget; S.E.T. and other tax increases expected to reduce demand by £200-£250m; but much larger turn round in government accounts.	
1970	.1378	.1362	Apr:	Budget; moderate direct-tax cuts aimed to boost demand by ½%, but little change in fiscal balance.	
			Nov:	Special Budget; further relaxation.	

In compressed form this table shows how deflationary measures actually do their work, and in particular it should be noted that every time there was a real crisis — nearly always in July because of the seasonal pattern in the balance of payments — the value of R slumped down over the next twelve months. Really poor values for R, following quite good ones for the previous period, are to be found after the deflationary measures taken in 1955, 1957, 1961, 1964/5, and 1968.

However it is, of course, a matter of simple logic that if deflation is known to restrict the rate of growth of the economy, it must reduce the value of R unless the amount of investment the previous year falls *pro rata* with the fall in output the current year, a state of affairs which one would have no good reason to expect. It should also be noted from the table above that higher levels of R are strongly associated year by year with rising levels of I although the reverse tendency is not so marked. However, in case there still should remain any doubt about the fact that deflation reduces the value of R, here is another table, this time correlating the changes in value of R upwards or downwards with changes in the number of unemployed lagged one year, as it is generally agreed that there is approximately a one year time lag between the effects of deflationary measures hitting demand and movements in the number of unemployed:

Table III.3

Year	R	R Up/Down	Unemployed Up/Down	U.K. Registered Unem'd (000's)	Year
1960	.3349			377	1961
1961	.2008	Down	Up	500	1962
1962	.0248	Down	Up	612	1963
1963	.3412	Up	Down	414	1964
1964	.4126	Up	Down	360	1965
1965	.1200	Down	Up	391	1966
1966	.1004	Down	Up	600	1967
1967	.1950	Up	Up	601	1968
1968	.2484	Up	Down	597	1969
1969	.0968	Down	Up		1970

This correlation is so marked as to need no further comment, and shows beyond doubt that policies of deflation not only waste investment, but also human resources as well.

There is one further point about Table III.2 which must be dealt with. Although inspection of the Table shows that years with high values of R tend to be years with rising values of I, when R fell I was inclined to drift downwards rather slowly. The result over the twenty years covered by the Table is that I rose from 9.5% in 1951 to 13.6% by 1970, although R was considerably higher during the early fifties than it was in the late sixties. This downwards stickiness of I has been one of the causes of the low average values for R during the last decade, and bears out again the futility of increasing investment while holding back demand. Taking Table III.2 and Table III.3 together shows the sad and bitter truth that increasing investment while holding demand down does not increase output, but does increase productivity which manifests itself in unemployment. What we really ought to be doing is ensuring that the productivity increases resulting from investment are used to increase the standard of living of our people, not to throw a rising proportion of them out of work.

What therefore emerges from this investigation is that the most important and significant way of increasing R, and thus total benefit, is not the micro economic process of increasing the potential productivity of investment, but ensuring that this potential is realised. This is an extremely important conclusion because it follows from it that the key to higher values for R is undoubtedly to have a high pressure of demand all the time, and that this is a far better prescription for more rapid rates of economic growth than all the available policies for increasing the potential efficiency of investment put together. It is also significant that rising values of R are also closely correlated in practice with rising values of I, so that the scene will be set for getting the cumulative benefit from raising both R and I together if a way can be devised of ensuring that the high pressure of demand required can be met without undue difficulties in other directions.

The Performance of Other O.E.C.D. Economies: Germany, France and Japan.

Before tackling this problem it would be worth while seeing what can in fact be achieved by looking at the performance of other countries. Tables III.4-7 show what has been happening in all OECD countries together, giving average figures for the whole of the developed world and then for three separate countries, two of them (Germany and France) in a fairly similar position to the U.K. These tables are all built up on exactly the same basis as Table III.1 so that the figures generally, and in particular the values for I and R, are comparable.

Taking Table III.4 first it is interesting to note both how relatively high and also how relatively consistent the value for R is. The average for the eleven years shown is .2751, a value which was only exceeded by Britain in four of those eleven years. The U.K. average for the same eleven years was .2199. The OECD average value for I is also a little higher than for Britain and also shows a more consistent tendency to rise. For the eleven year period the value for total benefit, adjusted for unemployment which was about 2.5%[9] and assuming no charge in the terms of trade is obtained as follows:

D	B
.90	11.62
.91	13.33
.92	15.59
.93	18.68
.94	23.15
.95	30.04
Unweighted average for total benefit	18.74
Unemployment Adjustment (5.0)	
Final Total Benefit	17.80

Table III.4

Summary of the Performance of all OECD Country Economics 1958-69

1	2	3	4	5	6	7	8
Year	GDP F-C	Capital Con-sumption	NDP F-C	GDCF	Increase St & WIP	5 + 6 Gross Invest-ment	7 – 3 Net Invest-ment
1958	819.9	84.5	735.4	169.3	7.0	176.3	91.8
1959	853.5	87.4	766.1	179.8	11.0	190.8	103.4
1960	888.5	91.5	797.0	189.2	14.6	203.8	112.3
1961	925.6	97.0	828.6	201.2	13.2	214.4	117.4
1962	976.6	104.6	872.0	215.3	13.7	229.0	124.4
1963	1021.5	110.1	911.4	226.1	13.5	239.6	129.5
1964	1084.0	117.8	966.2	247.4	16.5	263.9	146.1
1965	1143.6	124.4	1019.2	262.9	18.8	281.7	157.3
1966	1209.7	132.0	1077.7	278.8	21.6	300.4	168.4
1967	1251.5	139.9	1111.6	284.5	17.0	301.5	161.6
1968	1304.1	145.0	1159.1	300.8	21.6	322.4	177.4
1969	1363.9	151.6	1212.3	322.1	24.8	346.9	195.3
		1234.2		2555.3	168.5	2723.8	1489.6

Sources: *National Accounts of O.E.C.D. countries 1953-69,* published by O.E.C.D. *Labour Force Statistics 1958-69* published by O.E.C.D. All financial figures in billions of dollars at 1963 prices.

Tables III.5 and III.6, covering respectively Germany and France, present an interesting contrast. It will be noted that France had a slightly lower value for I but a much higher value for R than Germany had on average over the period. The main reason for this is the period of deflation which Germany went through during 1966 and 1967 producing values for R for these two years of .0968 and .0160, showing that Britain is by no means the only country which has suffered from this misfortune. The growth rates for the two countries during the period covered by the tables were 5.9% for France and 4.7% for Germany, despite the fact that both countries were investing about the same proportion of their national incomes. The obsession in Germany for avoiding inflation has been bought at a heavy cost in terms of

9	10	11	12	13	14	15	16
Year on Year Increase NDP-FC	Crude R	Total Working Pop. in Employment	Annual Increase	% Annual Increase	Actual R	N.N.P. F-C	8 as ratio 15 I
		258.7				738.1	.1243
30.7	.3344	261.2	2.5	.96	.2767	768.8	.1344
30.9	.2988	264.8	3.6	1.38	.2222	799.8	.1404
31.6	.2814	266.7	1.9	.72	.2431	831.8	.1411
43.4	.3697	269.5	2.8	1.05	.3141	876.2	.1419
39.4	.3167	271.4	1.9	.70	.2799	915.7	.1414
54.8	.4232	274.8	3.4	1.25	.3572	970.9	.1504
53.0	.3628	278.0	3.2	1.16	.3052	1024.2	.1535
58.5	.3719	281.7	3.7	1.33	.3073	1082.7	.1555
33.9	.2013	283.9	2.2	.78	.1639	1117.0	.1446
47.5	.2939	286.6	2.7	.95	.2449	1164.2	.1523
53.2	.2999	290.2	3.6	1.26	.2381	1217.2	.1604
476.9	.3202		31.5	12.18	.2751	10289.4	.1447

$$\Sigma B = \begin{array}{ll} D \\ .90 & 11.62 \\ .91 & 13.33 \\ .92 & 15.59 \\ .93 & 18.68 \\ .94 & 23.15 \\ .95 & 30.04 \end{array}$$

Average 18.74

growth — and this is reflected strongly in the values for total benefit shown below calculated on the usual basis:

D	Germany	France
.90	10.82	11.80
.91	12.44	13.64
.92	14.58	16.09
.93	17.51	19.49
.94	21.76	24.44
.95	28.35	32.19
Unweighted average for total benefit	17.58	19.61

Table III.5

Summary of the Performance of the German Economy 1960-69

1	2	3	4	5	6	7	8
Year	GDP F-C	Capital Con-sumption	NDP F-C	GDCF	Increase St & WIP	5 & 6 Gross Invest-ment	7 - 3 Net Invest-ment
1960	292.84	28.73	264.11	83.46	8.80	92.26	63.53
1961	309.00	31.35	277.65	91.67	6.70	98.37	67.02
1962	321.31	34.24	287.07	96.71	4.00	100.71	66.47
1963	333.71	37.19	296.52	99.06	2.10	101.16	63.97
1964	356.80	40.25	316.55	110.80	5.10	115.90	75.65
1965	378.59	43.63	334.96	115.89	9.50	125.39	81.76
1966	389.32	47.10	342.22	116.98	3.40	120.38	73.28
1967	386.13	50.23	335.90	107.17	−1.20	105.97	55.74
1968	418.06	53.39	364.67	115.65	11.00	126.65	73.26
1969	446.98	57.06	389.92	130.19	13.30	143.79	86.43
		366.11		937.39	49.4	986.79	620.68

Sources: *National Accounts of O.E.C.D. Countries 1953-1969* published by O.E.C.D. *Labour Force Statistics 1958-69* published by O.E.C.D. All financial figures in billions of DM at 1963 prices.

Unemployment in both countries was very low — about 1.0% in each case — and there were no significant changes in their terms of trade during the 60's. Adjusted total benefit for Germany was therefore 17.23 and for France 19.22. A further downward bias in the value of total benefit for Germany is required to account for the balance of payments surplus accrued during the period, which amounted to 2.7%[10] of Germany's national income during the period under review and 3.4%[10] of current consumption. Taking the view that these surpluses represent consumption foregone to no useful putpose, the value for Germany's total benefit should be reduced by 3.4%. However, as discussed in the previous chapter, this view seems too drastic, because surpluses do entail claims on resources, albeit in the future when they are subject both to inflation and factor *D*. Furthermore

9	10	11	12	13	14	15	16
Year on Year Increase NDP FC	Crude R	Total Working Pop. in Employment	Annual Increase	% Annual Increase	Actual R	N.N.P. F-C	8 Ratio to 15 I
		26,247				264.27	.2404
13.54	.2131	26,591	344	1.31	.1723	278.49	.2407
9.42	.1406	26,783	192	.72	.1182	287.88	.2309
9.45	.1422	26,880	97	.36	.1305	297.29	.2152
20.03	.3131	26,979	99	.37	.3003	317.77	.2381
18.41	.2434	27,153	174	.64	.2233	336.52	.2430
7.26	.0888	27,082	(71)	(.26)	.0968	343.54	.2133
(6.32)	(.0862)	26,292	(790)	(2.92)	.0160	337.31	.1652
28.77	.5161	26,343	51	.19	.5076	365.37	.2005
25.25	.3447	26,822	479	1.82	.2767	390.40	.2214
125.81	.2027		575	2.19	.1957	2828.44	.2194

$\quad\quad$ D
$\Sigma B =$ .90 10.82
$\quad\quad$ .91 12.44
$\quad\quad$ .92 14.58
$\quad\quad$ .93 17.51
$\quad\quad$ .94 21.76
$\quad\quad$ .95 28.35
Average 17.58

some of the surpluses did produce a return to the economy in the form of interest and dividends. Perhaps a fairer estimate would be to reduce total benefit by half the surplus as a proportion of consumption, i.e. 1.7%. This gives a final adjusted total benefit figure for Germany of 16.94. No such adjustment needs to be made for France.

It is of considerable interest to note that, although Germany has achieved a rate of growth closer to France's than to Britain's, whose average rate of growth over the same period was 2.8%, the value of total benefit for Germany is closer to that of Britain than the one for France. This points to the sophistication of total benefit as a measuring rod for the efficiency with which economies are run in that it discriminates between the real cost of the growth achieved by different countries depending on whether the emphasis has been on a relatively high rate of

Table III.6

Summary of the Performance of the French Economy 1959-69

1	2	3	4	5	6	7	8
Year	GDP F-C	Capital Con-sumption	NDP F-C	GDCF	Increase St & WIP	5 + 6 Gross Invest-ment	7 − 3 Net Invest-ment
1959	275.08	27.35	247.73	64.06	7.77	71.83	44.48
1960	295.52	29.88	265.64	69.00	13.41	82.41	52.53
1961	311.85	32.73	279.12	77.53	9.36	86.89	54.16
1962	332.75	36.07	296.68	84.66	11.39	96.05	59.98
1963	351.11	39.55	311.56	91.61	10.35	101.96	62.41
1964	372.70	43.16	329.54	104.27	11.26	115.53	72.37
1965	391.25	46.88	344.37	111.78	5.91	117.69	70.81
1966	413.38	51.03	362.35	121.13	10.59	131.72	80.69
1967	434.92	55.42	379.50	128.49	9.39	137.88	82.46
1968	462.20	59.83	402.37	136.96	6.68	143.64	83.81
1969	495.93	64.49	431.44	150.74	12.36	163.10	98.61
		421.90		989.49	96.11	1085.6	663.70

Sources: *National Accounts of O.E.C.D. countries 1953-69* published by O.E.C.D. *Labour Force Statistics 1958-69* published by O.E.C.D. All financial figures in billions of N.F. at 1963 prices.

investment with low returns, such as Germany, or a relatively low rate of investment and a high rate of return such as France.

Table III.7 shows what has been achieved in Japan during the last decade, and again there are some interesting and important lessons to be learnt. The most striking point is the average value of R attained combined with the high value of I, the optimum combination as we remarked earlier. However, unlike the French, the Japanese have not managed to avoid occasional severe deflations and 1965 saw a very poor value for R of .0824, and 1962 with a value for R of .1377 was, at least by Japanese standards, not much better. It is also noteworthy that the very high average values shown for R and I were achieved mainly by high values of R at the beginning of the period and high values of I at

9	10	11	12	13	14	15	16
Year on Year NDP-FC	Crude R	Total Working Pop. in Employment	Annual Increase	% Annual Increase	Actual R	N.N.P. F-C	8 Ratio to 15 I
		19,501				247.90	.1794
17.91	.4027	19,553	52	.27	.3914	265.59	.1978
13.48	.2566	19,554	1	.01	.2562	279.05	.1941
17.56	.3242	19,622	68	.35	.3107	296.15	.2025
14.88	.2481	19,818	196	1.00	.2110	310.93	.2007
17.98	.2881	20,058	240	1.21	.2428	328.83	.2201
14.83	.2049	20,128	70	.35	.1930	343.44	.2062
17.98	.2539	20,278	150	.75	.2266	361.33	.2233
17.15	.2125	20,340	62	.31	.2021	378.32	.2180
22.87	.2773	20,302	(38)	(.19)	.2839	401.61	.2087
29.07	.3469	20,530	228	1.12	.3065	:430.44:	.2291
183.71	.2768		1029	5.28	.2620	3213.15	.2066

$\Sigma B =$

D	
.90	11.80
.91	13.64
.92	16.09
.93	19.49
.94	24.44
.95	32.19
Average	19.61

the end. This is a very significant trend about which we shall have more to say later. The average growth rate for the Japanese economy between 1958 and 1969 was 11.2% per annum cumulatively, and the values for total benefit calculated on the usual basis are as follows:

D	
.90	13.45
.91	15.83
.92	19.06
.93	23.61
.94	30.39
.95	41.25
Unweighted average for total benefit	23.93

Table III.7

Summary of the Performance of the Japanese Economy 1958-69

1	2	3	4	5	6	7	8
Year	GDP F-C	Capital Con-sumption	NDP F-C	GDCF	Increase St & WIP	5 + 6 Gross Invest-ment	7 − 3 Net Invest-ment
1958	13,337	1429	11,908	3342	282	3,624	2,195
1959	14,576	1607	12,969	3830	457	4,287	2,680
1960	16,643	1863	14,780	5043	577	5,620	3,757
1961	19,248	2228	17,020	6468	1404	7,872	5,644
1962	20,488	2526	17,962	7164	393	7,557	5,031
1963	22,659	2855	19,804	7875	884	8,759	5,904
1964	25,700	3362	22,338	9219	1097	10,316	6,954
1965	26,824	3643	23,181	9426	728	10,154	6,511
1966	29,487	4111	25,376	10,540	980	11,520	7,409
1967	33,349	4631	28,718	12,448	2149	14,597	9,966
1968	38,120	5227	32,893	15,123	2309	17,432	12,205
1969	42,869	6112	36,757	17,894	2409	20,303	14,191
		33,482		90,478	11,260	101,738	68,256

Sources: *National Accounts of O.E.C.D. Countries 1953-69* published by O.E.C.D. *Labour Force Statistics* 1958-69 published by O.E.C.D. All financial figures in billions of year at 1963 prices.

This figure is not subject to much adjustment. The Japanese terms of trade did not alter appreciably during the period. They ran a negligible balance of payments surplus on current account (414 million yen out of a total national income during the period of 227,575 million yen)[11] and unemployment was of the order of 1%. Making this adjustment only gives a final total benefit figure for Japan of 23.45. It is also very interesting to note that according to the values for I_{opt} given in the last chapter Japan, with a value for R of .3400, is investing just about the optimum with a value for I of .2999, whereas all the other countries we have looked at are well below this optimum percentage.

It is, of course, true that the values for total benefit obtained during

9	10	11	12	13	14	15	16
Year on Year Increase NDP-FC	Crude R	Total Working Pop. in Employment	Annual Increase	% Annual Increase	Actual R	N.N.P. F-C	8 Ratio to 15 I
		42,980				11,918	.1842
1,061	.4834	43,350	370	.86	.4484	12,989	.2063
1,811	.6757	44,360	1010	2.33	.5912	14,808	.2537
2,240	.5962	44,980	620	1.40	.5549	17,066	.3307
942	.1669	45,560	580	1.29	.1377	18,015	.2787
1,842	.3661	45,950	390	.86	.3431	19,871	.2971
2,534	.4292	46,550	600	1.31	.3962	22,430	.3100
843	.1212	47,300	750	1.61	.0824	23,261	.2799
2,195	.3371	48,270	970	2.05	.2824	25,448	.2911
3,342	.4511	49,200	930	1.93	.4015	28,785	.3462
4,175	.4189	50,020	820	1.67	.3828	32,984	.3700
3,864	.3166	50,400	380	.76	.3012	36,844	.3851
24,849	.3641		7420	17.26	.3415	227,575	.2999

$$\Sigma B = \begin{array}{cc} & D \\ .90 & 13.45 \\ .91 & 15.83 \\ .92 & 19.06 \\ .93 & 23.61 \\ .94 & 30.39 \\ .95 & 41.25 \end{array}$$

Average 23.93

the last few pages are by themselves meaningless, but the comparative values for different countries are highly significant in that they provide a comprehensive measurement of the efficiency with which their economies are being run. Using this yardstick it is now possible to construct a new 'league table' and the figures obtained so far are as follows:

Japan	23.45	132
France	19.22	108
OECD Average	17.80	100
Germany	16.94	95
Britain	15.71	88

The last column shows these performance figures raised to index numbers based on the OECD average as 100. The overall performance obtained from Britain's economy is thus shown to be 12% worse than the OECD average on the total benefit measurement scale, while Japan, which is somewhere near an optimum position, is 32% better than the OECD average.

The Essence of the Problem with the British Economy

The problem now to be investigated is what can be done to achieve higher values of total benefit for Britain, bearing in mind all the points which have been gathered together in the analysis so far. It has already emerged clearly that by far the most efficacious way of raising total benefit is to increase the values of both I and R together, but we are also in a position to assess the effects on the same maximand of any reductions in benefit caused by other policy goals not being achieved because of side effects of raising R and I. The procedure to be adopted, therefore, is to concentrate in the first instance on what can be done to increase values of R and I, and then to consider how far and how fast a policy of this sort can be pushed before the benefits start being outweighed by the loss of benefit in other directions. It is also, of course, vital that the practical political parameters within which the policy has got to be made to work should be borne in mind all the time. These involve not only domestic political and social restraints, but also international obligations which must be countenanced.

Inspection of Tables III.1, 4, 5, 6 and 7 shows that high values of R and I tend to be associated when comparing different economies, and we have already noted that in the British economy rising values of I tend to coincide with high values of R. It is also not surprising that high growth rates are also associated with high values of R and I, since the product of R and I is a more or less exact measurement of the rate of growth which economies are achieving. The reason for values of R, I and hence rates of growth moving together are not hard to come by. A high rate of economic growth implies that there has not been too much deflation, which depresses R more than anything else as we have already seen. We have also noted that deflation depresses I, because low rates of social return, of which R is the measure, must necessarily be correlated with low rates of private return and hence a climate of opinion which is not conducive to investment. On the other hand high values for R imply that investment is very profitable for those who undertake it, therefore encouraging a higher value for I and hence cumulatively higher growth rates. Furthermore there are good reasons for believing that high values for I in themselves tend to produce higher values for R and hence more growth still for at least two good reasons. The first is that as I gets larger the proportion of investment undertaken which is in manufacturing, as against social investment in housing and public utilities, tends to rise, and as manufacturing investment generally has a higher social rate of return the average value for R gets pulled up[1][2] Second, high values for I, particularly over a long period of time, have a cumulative effect in making the economy especially well adapted both to market opportunities throughout the world and to technological advances, thus again raising R.

On the other hand it is of course only too familiar a spectacle to see low values for R, I and rates of economic growth going together. These correlations are well known in the form of the virtuous and vicious circle metaphors, and many efforts have been made during the last two decades to break out of the vicious circle which Britain is certainly in. It is important to investigate the methods which have been tried so far and to see why they have failed before going on to put forward different proposals and explain why they should succeed. In essence there are three ways of tackling the problem: one can generate boom conditions via reflation and hope that R and I rise sufficiency quickly to make the boom self sustaining; one can try to improve the efficiency of the investment which is being made and so try to raise the value of R directly; and one can try to increase the amount of investment being done and thus raise I directly. Let us look at each of these policies in turn, bearing in mind that they are not in any way mutually exclusive and may well be used in combination with each other.

Why the Solutions tried up to now have failed

Reflation as a solution to the problem has been tried on several occasions during the last two decades, and in particular it was tried by Reginald Maudling during the period 1963/4, and it is being tried now by Anthony Barber. Since attempts to stimulate investment directly have not been successful for reasons to be discussed shortly, and since the export market has to be regarded as datum with the present foreign exchange arrangements, the only way of reflating is to increase consumer demand. This can be done by reducing taxation, relaxing hire purchase restrictions and bank lending ceilings, and so on. Consumer led booms take a few months to gather steam and they do for a short period lead to somewhat higher values of both R and I. However, the reason why they have always failed, and why there is no doubt that the Barber boom will fail as well in the end, is that once the slack in the economy is taken up, the volume of extra output which can be generated from the amount of investment being undertaken, with any conceivable value for R, is just too low to deal with the consumer expectations caused by the boom conditions. The main reason why this is so is that consumer booms gather momentum quite quickly whereas investment programmes generally take considerably longer to alter. By the time new plans for investment have been drawn up the boom may well be making resources for investment rather hard to come by, and with balance of payments problems on the horizon, and signs of overheating in the offing industrialists may well tend to take the view that investment projects actually ordered at this point are likely to be installed just as the boom finishes. Having been caught several times before during the last few years they are understandably very cautious. What is wrong with consumer led booms is the timing. Domestic expectations are raised before the productive capacity is made available to meet them, and as a result what tends to happen is that consumer demand precipitates a rise in imports in relation to exports causing a balance of payments crisis. Because industrialists know this they are even more cautious over investment plans. The remedy then applied is deflation bringing the policy of relation to an end. The quantitative aspects of this analysis are very important and they will be discussed later on when we consider what is likely to happen to the British economy in detail if present policies continue, but the general conclusion that consumer led booms are no answer to the problem must stand.

The second possibility is to try to do something directly about R, and there are a great many different policies which have been pursued by the goverment over the last twenty years with this objective in mind. These have involved everything from restructuring British industry via the I.R.C. and other pressures, to improving methods of applying the results of government research in industry. While there is no doubt that some of these policies have increased the potential value of R — though we shall argue later that others have done precisely the opposite — it is not the potential value of R which is critical so much as the actual value obtained, and, as we have seen already, this is far more a function of the pressure of demand that anything else. What is true is that high potential values for R certainly may enable consumer led booms to last longer before they run into inflation and balance of payments troubles and in this respect direct action to increase the potential value of R is well worth while. However, the government's ability to achieve this objective turns very much on correct judgement as to what does actually increase potential R, and when we get on to this subject a little later we shall find that the present yardsticks used are by no means appropriate. Thus the conclusions we arrive at here are, first, that it is not potential but actual R which is important, and this is a function much more of pressure of demand than of the efficiency of the investment which is being carried out, and, secondly, that while there should be a role for the government to play in increasing potential R, and thus actual R given the right demand conditions, this role depends very much on different investment appraisal methods being used than those which are currently employed.

The third possible way of breaking out of the vicious circle is to try to do something about I directly, and the problem again is to find a policy which will actually work. At one time it was thought that reducing interest rates would make investment more profitable and thus raise the amount undertaken, but innumerable studies have shown that interest rates are a negligible element in most appraisals of investment profitability, more particularly in inflationary conditions. Their influence on decisions is almost non-existent except in the case of very long lasting low yield investment such as residential construction. More recently attempts have been made to increase investment by grants. The problem with them is that they do very little to encourage investment which is profitable anyway, the type which really does increase potential R, but they do encourage unprofitable investment, thus using up scarce investment resources on projects which may well have a negligible potential contribution to make to R even in the most happy circumstances of high pressure of demand. Investment grants have considerable advantage in a social sense in providing a more reasonable balance of industry and employment between the regions of Britain, but they do not have much of a role to play in increasing I with a reasonable R potential. The latest system of allowing more rapid write off of investment against profits at least has the merit of encouraging profitable projects, though unfortunately it apparently puts a greater strain than it is able to bear on many companies' ability to calculate what is to their best post-tax advantage, quite apart from its socially regressive qualities regarding the regions. However, no one expects these depreciation allowances to make a really major change in the situation.

Another method of encouraging investment which was tried during the Labour administration was a version of indicative planning. The idea was to have a National Plan showing what investment would be required by all sectors of the economy, and then to encourage everyone to invest together to achieve the targets set. Unfortunately the National Plan was based on excessively optimistic calculations about the balance of payments prospects of the economy at the time and therefore one of the major preconditions of success for this type of Plan, a stable balance of payments, was removed before the Plan began to be put into effect. This meant that all the effect the Plan had was to encourage investment which was surplus to requirements, e.g. in the Central Electricity Generating Board.[13] As a consequence this type of planning has been discredited for a while ahead.

Yet another possibility for increasing I is for the government to undertake investment itself in default of private industry being prepared to do so. This policy has certainly been followed to a substantial extent, but it is an unfortunate fact that by and large the projects which the government has undertaken either within the public sector, or in association with industry, have been ones with a relatively small potential contribution to R. Again the reasons for this state of affairs must be left until later when the question of investment appraisal is undertaken in a systematic fashion, and it may well be possible to improve the results from government investment, but certainly on the criteria used up till now increasing I by direct government action is only too likely to lower the value of R so that the gain to total benfit is very small.

In sum, all these ways of bribing, exhorting or ordering industry in the public or private sectors to undertake more investment have two major failings. First they have all been tried and they have all either not been very successful, or they have failed together so that no one now seriously believes that any of them is going to make any major difference to the present situation. Second none of them gets to the core of what both makes people want to invest more and also makes more investment worthwhile from the point of view of the whole economy, and this is a certainty that once the investment has been made it is going to be used to the full. The key to increasing I is not tinkering about with interest rates or taxes, or persuasion or any sort of direct action to get investment undertaken, which is in grave danger of being under-utilised or not really required, it is to provide the assurance .of sustained high levels of demand so that investment undertaken can be guaranteed high utilisation. We have seen already that these are also precisely the conditions which lead to high values of R. Thus the solution to the problem of breaking out of the vicious circle is to find a policy which will enable a high level of demand to be sustained, which starts off by increasing I and R before consumer demand pre-empts too many resources, which will not run into balance of payments restraints, and whose impact on inflation and its consequences will not bring back down again the much higher value of total benefit which would otherwise be obtained. This policy must also be within acceptable political and social limits. A policy which will do all these things is perfectly feasible and it begins with a different exchange rate policy to the one which Britain has pursued up till now.

Undervaluation — A New Policy for Growth

Until recently the policy of the U.K. has been to defend the parity of the pound at more or less any cost, and to regard any devaluation which had to take place as a major political defeat, whatever disclaimers may have been made at the time. We have, however, seen in the last chapter that in terms of total benefit this policy has nothing to recommend it whatsoever. Recently with the dollar float, the pound floated for a while too, introducing a little more flexibility, and this is a step in the right direction because at least it means that the parity of the pound can be made to change gradually, although the authorities have not yet made much effort to use this freedom. They have been very much inclined to take a very cautious view and to hold sterling as close as possible to previous parities; indeed for some periods the pound has actually been above its previous parity in relation to the currencies of the rest of the world. In sum, the latest developments have involved a little more flexibility than there was previously, but no really major departure from previous parities and no great likelihood of any taking place in the near future.

What is proposed here as a first step to solving Britain's economic problems is a much more radical policy than this. Rather than treat the present parity of the pound as an objective in itself, or even as a way of balancing supply and demand for sterling, the proposal now put forward is that the external value of the pound should be used as a major policy weapon on its own account. We should devalue the pound by a really substantial amount, 20% seeming to be about the optimum figure, and then float to get the benefits of flexibility, but making sure that the pound is not allowed to float back upwards again, at least for the time being. We should adopt an exchange rate policy of reducing interest rates right down, perhaps following the French example of having two exchange markets, one for trade and the other for other financial transactions. A policy of this sort would have one major advantage, and several substantial disadvantages, and we must now investigate these in turn.

The major advantage is that a devaluation of this sort does not just make up for competitiveness already lost because of more inflation here than elsewhere. Nor does it strive to achieve equilibrium at whatever level of economic activity there is at the moment. What it sets out to do quite deliberately is to produce some degree of disequilibrium, at least temporarily, while the process of raising I and R is going on. When this process is complete the time for equilibrium will have arrived again. The object of this policy is to generate precisely the conditions outlined for raising total benefit, namely an export led investment boom, leading to much higher values of both R and I in conditions which can be sustained. Why will this boom take place? The reason is that almost the whole of industry will have a virtually cast iron guarantee of profitable outlets for the foreseeable future overseas, if not within Britain, although the very boom conditions themselves will inevitably lead to rapidly rising domestic prosperity. However, as the demand leading to the boom will be export led it will not be necessary to get into the situation which has dogged the U.K. for so long of pre-empting resources via consumer demand. By the time consumer demand does pick up, the resources will be able to meet it both in terms of increased domestic output, and in terms of increased capacity to import because of increased exports. All this needs very careful quantifications, which will be carried out shortly, but it is worth noting at this stage that all the economies — Japan's in particular — which have done really well since the war have had undervalued currencies to start them off on rapid growth, so that there is considerable *prima facie* evidence that an undervalued currency policy as a temporary measure is likely to be successful. The only interesting exception to this rule was France, where rather different circumstances to those applying in Britain allowed her to generate a high level of domestic demand and then devalue later to solve the balance of payment problems which overtook her. However, Britain is much more dependant than France on world trade, particularly for raw materials, and so there are good reasons for disallowing this as a special case.

We must now investigate the disadvantages of pursuing a policy of having a deliberately undervalued currency for a period of time and see how substantial these disadvantages turn out to be. The main points to be considered are first that this policy is contrary to our international obligations, second that other countries will take retaliatory action against us, third that devaluation will turn the terms of trade against us and thus make us worse off than we were before, fourth that devaluation will lead to more domestic inflation, and finally that the sterling balances present an insuperable obstacle to the policy proposed.

As regards our obligations to the international community, and the I.M.F. in particular, the criterion to be applied to a currency which is in line for devaluation is that it should be fundamentally out of alignment with parities in the rest of the world for this course of action to be justified. It is the contention in this book that this condition does apply to Britain, but that the current methods of judging whether a currency is undervalued or not are based on the wrong criteria. The main criterion employed has been the state of the balance of payments, but the argument deployed in these pages is very much to the effect that this is by no means the only, and far from the most important or relevant, yardstick for judging an economy's state of health. Indeed, the very yardstick put forward in the analysis developed in the last chapter, total benefit, is far more appropriate. This is a far more rational criterion to adopt, and we must fight for its acceptance. In particular we should be on our guard against those countries such as Germany who put low levels of inflation in the forefront of their policy objectives (which we have seen is not a rational policy at all), and other countries who are likely to oppose any scheme which is based on the premise advanced here that a low value for total benefit should be the criterion used for deciding whether a currency is ripe for devaluation or not. There really is a limit to the extent to which we can allow ourselves to get caught more and more firmly in the vicious spiral of slow growth because of irrational or beggar-my-neighbour policies pursued elsewhere.

If it is argued that it is unreasonable for us to devalue because we are running a current account surplus we must point out that we are only doing so at the cost of massive deflation and a stagnant economy. There are not many people who now believe that we could reflate our economy without running into a balance of payments problem again unless we devalue at some stage. The argument here is that we ought to devalue early so that the reflation can be export led, rather than devalue later on after a domestically led boom when already too many resources have been deployed into consumption.

The main objections to one country devaluing its currency as seen by all the other countries in the world are first that the devaluing country's exports get more competitive, and second that it may aim to improve its balance of payments position at every other country's expense. Now it may well be true that devaluing countries have, in the past, had precisely these objectives in mind, but it does not follow that devaluation will always produce these results. In fact the aim of devaluation as proposed here is not to make Britain's exports more competitive so much as to make them more profitable for domestic producers to export rather than sell internally. If Britain can export quite reasonable quantities of goods and services at present price levels there is no good reason to believe that export prices would fall all that much in terms of foreign currencies after devaluation; they would merely rise sharply in terms of domestic currency. On the import side, similar arguments apply. The object of devaluation is not to import less, and indeed quite the opposite is certain to happen, as we shall see when we consider in detail what a budget for Britain for the next five years would look like after devaluation. Nor is it likely that there would be much reduction in the prices of U.K. imports in terms of external currencies; it is far more likely that there will be substantial domestic price rises for imported products – a problem which we will have to consider shortly. Thus the dislocation to foreign suppliers and competitors is not likely to be very great, and it is extremely difficult to see how the cost of this dislocation cannot be offset many times over by having a really booming British economy, importing far more of the rest of the world's exports than previously, which is precisely what we should aim to have happening.

As regards the argument that by devaluing we aim to improve our balance of payments position and upset everyone else by running up surpluses, we should give an unequivocal declaration that we have not the slightest intention of doing any such thing. Running up balance of payments surpluses is thoroughly irrational as a policy objective and one which we certainly ought to avoid. In fact as we shall see shortly increasing I, in particular, involves using all the resources available, and squandering any of these on balance of payments surpluses unnecessarily would be the height of folly. Once acceptable values of R and I had been attained, if there were any tendency for the U.K. to accumulate surpluses, they should be disposed of as fast as possible by revaluing the currency or by reducing import tariffs. There is no reason why our policy objectives in all these respects should not be made quite clear at the outset, and one would hope that in these circumstances the international objections to the policy proposed would at least be rather more muted than they might otherwise be. However, in the last analysis, if we cannot convince enough of the international financial community of our basic good intent, and in particular that the policy we wish to pursue is not one of beggar-my-neighbour, but in practice exactly the opposite, then we will have to go ahead and devalue without their approval. But which is worse, stagnation and a million unemployed, or the disapproval of the I.M.F.?

This leads on to the second consideration which is whether other countries would retaliate against our devaluing. There are two ways in which this could happen; one would be for other countries to devalue with us, and the other would be for tariff barriers to be erected against us. Provided the reasons for our devaluation were made clear, and in particular our policy with regard to export prices, imports and surpluses were spelled out, there is no reason to believe that the amount of devaluations which would follow ours would be all that great at least among the countries in the developed world. We are about the same size as France as a trading nation, and France has devalued several times without major repercussions. We have also devalued twice ourselves since the war. The countries who may devalue with us are our principle raw material suppliers, particularly for foodstuffs. However this is a matter to be welcomed rather than the reverse. Ideally what we want is for those countries which supply us with raw materials to devalue with us, so that these import prices do not rise, while our main industrial competitors do not, thus allowing us to raise export prices in terms of domestic currency for industrial exports. In the past these happy circumstances have tended to eventuate, but our impending entry into the Common Market is going to make this aspect of our affairs considerably more difficult, because the Common Agricultural Policy effectively ties our food import prices to those reigning inside the E.E.C., which are higher than those of our existing suppliers such as New Zealand and Denmark, and the whole devaluation policy will have failed if they all devalue with us. This is a matter which we shall have to consider in more detail when we review the effects on total benefit for the U.K. of our joining the Common Market.

Likewise the chance of other countries putting up tariff barriers against us are minimal. In the first place discriminatory tariffs of this sort are totally against both the spirit and the letter of GATT, secondly they are cumbersome to enforce, and thirdly Britain's share of world trade is now just not large enough to warrant that much concern over what we do. We can rely on any retaliation of this sort being easily surmountable.

Our third consideration over devaluation is that we make ourselves worse off by devaluing. It is of course true that import prices rise because of devaluation, but it is a total fallacy to assume from this that the economy as a whole, and therefore all the people who compose it, are necessarily worse off at all as a result of devaluation. While it is true that import prices rise in terms of the domestic currency, so do export prices and it may well be that the one will not only offset the other but may actually overcompensate for any losses on the import side. The critical factor is what happens to the terms of trade. If these worsen as a result of devaluation then the economy as a whole is worse off, but if they improve then the economy as a whole is actually better off. What would happen if we devalued would turn entirely on the circumstances of the time, and there is nothing which can determine what the effects would be *a priori*. Experience in the past has tended to suggest that the change in import prices and export prices has been broadly similar so that the terms of trade have not altered appreciably at all.[14] However, in the past we have had the benefit of having our main food suppliers devaluing with us, a benefit we would lose once we are inside the Common Market, so that in this respect we might be rather worse off than before. In general, however, it does seem that there is nothing to fear on this score. Where there is a problem, however, is that in the first instance most of the costs of rising imports hit those on wages and salaries, while most of the benefits from increased exports go to increase company profits. However, there is no reason why the process of wage increases or the tax system should not be used to compensate for this movement against the redistribution of income, and in any case there is a further consideration: if British companies simply pay out increased profits to their shareholders the case of mulcting them may be strong, but if we are positing an investment boom then the money to pay for all the increased investment has got to come from somewhere. The profits of British industry over the last decade have been exceedingly low by international standards, and perhaps this is not very important in so far as there has not been the requirement for more investment because of lack of demand. Therefore although British companies' profits have been low, they have had adequate funds for all the investment which was worth undertaking.[15] However, this situation will change sharply with a real investment boom and therefore higher company profits, provided they are used for investment and not for paying out to shareholders is in everyone's interest. Increasing profits by making exports more profitable – and import substitutes too – is one way of doing this, and, as we shall see when we get down to budgeting, we shall still be able to afford substantial real increases to wage and salary earners even after allowing for the effects of rising import prices so hat everyone will be better off.

We must now turn to the question of the amount of extra inflation caused by devaluation. The first point to be made is that all the analysis in Chapter II suggested that inflation is not such an evil *per se*, and that if a choice has to be made between either more growth and less unemployment, or inflation, then we ought to accept more inflation as a price to pay for higher rates of growth and fuller employment. However it must be recognised that many people do not like inflation, so we must investigate how much extra inflation is likely to be caused by the devaluation policy proposed, and we must also look at the more substantive point which is that high rates of inflation may affect R.

The inflationary impact of devaluation can be quantified fairly easily in the first instance. If roughly 30% of inputs are imported, and if we devalue by 20% and have to absorb the whole of this amount in the form of price increases, then the total price increases would be 20% x 30% which is 6% in the first instance. However some import substitute prices will rise too, and in practice foreign suppliers will absorb some of the domestic price rise. Let us assume the one effect here balances out the other. Past experience suggests that there are time lags of about three months before increased import prices work their way through to retail prices, and about six months before the price increases cause ensuing wage claims which keep the inflationary spiral going.[16] Most wage increases are on an annual basis – at least those which are centrally negotiated. As time goes on the impact of an inflationary impact tends to die down, each subsequent round of price and wage increases being roughly half the previous one. Thus a very rough guess at the additional amount of inflation which would result from the devaluation policy proposed would be about 6% in the first year, about

3% in the second year, and about 1½% in the third year, i.e. just over 10% in the first three years. However, this inflation is measured before other factors are introduced which may well reduce the inflationary impact considerably. In the past when there have been devaluations these have been accompanied by deflation on the grounds that only deflation would make way for the necessary exports to make the devaluation policy work. With this premise it was necessary for there to be virtually no increase in domestic consumption, so that all the impetus from import price increases tended to raise prices in a purely inflationary manner; in particular wage and salary increases were not accompanied by any growth in output to absorb their inflationary consequences. However, the policy proposed in this book is entirely different in that the object of the devaluation should be to raise R and I sufficiently rapidly both to make way for increased exports and investment and to generate some increase in real output for consumption, which will thus go at least some of the way to absorbing the inflationary impact of devaluation. However, even if this were not so, it must be baldly stated that we would definitely be better off with an extra 10% inflation over a three year period if, by accepting this, we could have a much higher rate of growth and less unemployment. If the choice has to be made the inflationary price must be paid.

Supposing that there is a good deal of extra inflation, will R be adversely affected to a point where the gains to R from boom conditions are lost? To this question an absolutely unequivocal answer can be given. The gains to R from a high pressure of demand are so very substantial, and the losses to R so relatively small from any level of inflation which we would conceivably experience, that there is no shadow of doubt that R would increase and not decrease post devaluation even if there was more inflation than is anticipated here.

There is one further very important matter to be considered, which is another aspect of our international obligations, and this relates to the large sums of money owed by the British government and other private individuals and corporations denominated in sterling. These sterling liabilities have been a major problem, and their existence was one of the most important factors in putting off previous devaluations. It is of course true that some of these liabilities, particularly those relating to sterling's reserve currency role, are now guaranteed in dollars or DM as a result of the Basle Agreement so that there is no moral or practical problem as far as they are concerned. Nevertheless, there still remains a very large sum of money in aggregate[17] whose value in international terms would go down by some 20% overnight if devaluation were announced out of the blue. However merely stating the problem in this form goes half way to suggesting how this problem would in fact be solved. Whatever else one may consider probable, it is extremely unlikely that the undervalued currency policy advocated here is going to be adopted overnight. What is far more likely to happen is that what we shall henceforward refer to as the New Policy would only gradually become accepted as a result of a campaign of persuasion. However, as more people become persuaded, so the policy would in fact become self fulfilling. If it became clear that a large number of people either in the government, or in the opposition which might well become the government shortly, were determined to see a policy of undervaluation put into effect, then the parity of sterling would start to fall. If the currency were floating, then it would float down; if it were pegged, then the peg would give way and it would still come down, only this time rather more quickly after a futile attempt to prop it up. This very process of the parity coming down in a reasonably gentle manner would give everyone time to adjust to the new situation. Those who adjust more quickly would benefit as against those who did so more slowly, but this is no new situation. All those involved in financial affairs are used to far greater changes in prices than ones of 20% — in share prices and commodities to state only two examples — so there is no reason why a 20% change in the parity of the pound taking place over a period of perhaps a year or two should upset them unduly. Thus a policy of floating the pound down by a substantial amount is found to be both much easier and far less liable to cause dislocation or moral opprobrium than an overnight devaluation. It therefore gets over most of the difficulties which have held back governments from a policy of devaluation in the past. However, to ensure that this float down to what is in the first instance a position of deliberate disequilibrium takes place, it is essential for there to be enough people determined to see this happen, if necessary by overnight devaluation, before the self fulfilling element, which in fact takes the sting out, will manifest itself. It should also be noted that this gradual move to undervaluation will also give other countries time to adjust to what is going on as it happens, and the very fact that it does not happen in one immediate administrative step is more than likely to mute objections to the policy being pursued.

Parameters for a New Policy Budget

We are now getting close to the point where we can begin to construct a budget for the U.K. for the next few years showing what could be done, but before embarking on this exercise there is one point which must be covered concerning the starting date for our New Policy as against the type of policy which is being employed at the moment. Advocating a policy to be applied starting at some date in the future has the major drawback that it is impossible to be certain of exactly what the conditions at the start are going to be, and therefore any prescriptions are difficult to relate back in detail to the actual situation. To get over this problem the procedure adopted in this chapter is to assume that the policy proposals advocated were put into effect on 1st January 1971, and the results are then followed through in detail for a five year period until the end of 1975. We are thus starting from the published figures relating to the state of the British economy at the end of 1970 as set out in the 1971 National Income and Expenditure Blue Book. This makes it possible to produce definite budget proposals for the five year period showing clearly how our major objectives should be achieved and related back to the actual conditions which obtained only a short time ago. Obviously by the time the proposals in this book are published the situation will have changed and some variations in prescription will be necessary, and these are discussed later on in this chapter. A definite starting date like 1st January 1971 has two further advantages: in the first place it makes it possible to construct a similar parallel budget to that for the New Policy showing what is likely to happen if present policies are continued, and in the second place the very fact that by the time this book is in the reader's hands we will already be falling badly behind in almost all respects in relation to what is advocated here points up the urgency of the situation more clearly than any discussion based on hypothetical starting points in the future.

Before beginning to construct this five year New Policy budget it is also worth going over again the main premises upon which this policy is based and noting the restraints within which it has got to be made to work. The first objective is to use an export led investment boom to produce simultaneously a high value of R with a rising value of I. Since there are also unused resources in the economy in the form of unemployment of both labour and capital equipment, we can rely on some extra output from these sources as well. We must then ensure that R

is not allowed to fall back because of deflation so that *I* can continue to rise — the old virtuous circle. To avoid deflation the balance of payments position must be watched very carefully, and in particular we must ensure that there is enough output from the domestic economy to enable all claims put upon it to be met without excess demand sucking in more imports than we can afford to pay for. This objective is particularly difficult to attain if we want to try very hard to have at least some increase in the real standard of living even during the first year of the New Policy — no doubt an important element politically in getting this policy accepted. Finally we must look very carefully at what would happen if our estimates are materially wrong in any or all respects, so that we can see what the consequences of wrong estimation are likely to be and what further resources or policy measures might be pressed then into service to put matters right again.

Part 3   New Policy Proposals

New Policy Budget 1 — An Export Led Investment Boom

Table III.8 shows an overall five year budget for the U.K. based on what could have been achieved with the situation as it was at the end of 1970. The 1970 figures are therefore actual and those from 1971-75 are conjectural. All the figures presented are at 1970 prices with no allowance made for inflation. Obviously there will be some inflation during all the years from 1971-75 so that the figures in money terms for all these years would be higher. However, the ratios between different sums making up the total would not alter appreciably and it is easier to see what is happening in constant prices. It is posited that if the rate of inflation were higher in Britain than overseas, the external value of sterling could be allowed to float down accordingly so that British domestic prices would remain where they were in relation to prices elsewhere in the world; in other words the benefits of devaluation would not be allowed to be whittled away by domestic inflation. Let us now consider this five year budget section by section.

   The proposal is that on 1st January 1971 what we have called the New Policy is adopted, and the external value of sterling is made to drop as quickly as possible by about 20%. This could happen by an

Table III.8

1970-1975 BUDGET – NEW POLICY
All Financial Figures in £m at 1970 prices

	1970	1971	1972	1973	1974	1975
GNP – FC	42,819	45,097	48,172	51,003	54,069	57,435
Less: Capital Consumption	4,132	4,339	4,560	4,797	5,051	5,324
NNP – FC	38,687	40,758	43,612	46,206	49,018	52,111
Less: Net Property						
Income from Abroad	512	500	500	500	500	500
NDP F-C	38,175	40,258	43,112	45,706	48,518	51,611
Made up of						
% Increase Net Inv.		25%	20%	20%	10%	10%
Net Investment	5,208	6,510	7,812	9,374	10,311	11,342
Exports G & S	11,182	12,771	14,365	15,592	16,799	17,989
Less Imports G & S	10,898	12,850	14,245	15,847	17,009	18,442
Consumption	32,683	33,827	35,180	36,587	38,417	40,722
	38,175	40,258	43,112	45,706	48,518	51,611
% Increase Consumption p.a.		3.5%	4.0%	4.0%	5.0%	6.0%
Balance of Trade		(79)	120	(255)	(210)	(453)
Balance of Payments Current A/C	421	620	245	290	47
Exports as % GNP		28.32%	29.82%	30.57%	31.07%	31.32%
Calculations re Next Year						
Last Year's Investment		5208	6510	7812	9374	10,311
Estimated Value for *R*		.4	.4	.3	.3	.3
Extra NDP – FC this year from *R*		2083	2604	2344	2812	3093
Increase from Extra Employment			250	250		
Last Year's NDP – FC		38,175	40,258	43,112	45,706	48,518
This Year's NDP – FC		40,258	43,112	45,706	48,518	51,611
Add: Net Property Income from		500	500	500	500	500
Abroad Capital Consumption		4339	4560	4797	5,051	5,324
Total this year's GNP – FC		45,097	48,172	51,003	54,069	57,435
I	.1346	.1597	.1791	.2029	.2104	.2177
R	.1378	.4000	.4000	.3000	.3000	.3000
% Increase GNP	1.59	5.32	6.82	5.88	6.01	6.23

overnight devaluation, though as we have already seen it is much more likely that there would have been a float down. The first objective of this policy is to make exporting in domestic currency very much more profitable and thus to switch effort to the export market. While no doubt there would be a certain amount of price cutting in external currency, wherever possible exporters should be encouraged to keep their prices up unless they really needed to drop them. On the import side it is likely that foreign suppliers would cut their prices a bit to maintain their market shares in Britain, but again the main emphasis should go on encouraging import competing industries to become more profitable. Assuming that the changes in import and export prices are roughly the same, there will be no material change in the terms of trade and thus no loss to the economy as a whole from this direction. To find out what is actually likely to happen to exports and imports as percentages of the Gross National Product, the most suitable measure in this particular case since replacement investment involves imports, Tables III.9 A, B and C show in some detail the trends that have occurred over the last ten years covering the period of the last devaluation at the end of 1967. What had been done is to show imports and exports as percentages of the Gross National Product year by year with annual measures beside them of the major factors likely to influence these import and export percentages. By taking periods as long as a year it is felt that the worst effects of special factors such as dock strikes can be ironed out. The main factors likely to influence the proportion of Gross National Product devoted to imports and exports have been taken to be the following:

1. The rate of inflation in Britain compared with the rest of the OECD countries, our main competitors. This has been computed by taking the OECD deflator for all OECD countries and comparing it with the U.K. deflator. This was felt to be a better measure of the true pressure on imports and exports than import and export prices since it is believed that it is the profitability of imports and exports which is the crucial factor in trying to determine which way trends will move.
2. The growth of all OECD trade.
3. The growth of the British Gross National Product.

The rates of change of each of these factors is shown year by year, and at the bottom of the table are shown the correlations between the rates of change of imports and exports as percentages of the Gross

Table III.9A

IMPORT AND EXPORT RATIOS – Goods and Services
Based on Curent Prices

Year	UK Imports as % GNP-FC	Increase as % GNP-FC UK Imports on Previous Year	Deflator Measure Loss Competi-tiveness	% Growth all OECD Trade	% Growth UK GNP-FC	Increase as % GNP-FC UK Exports on Previous Year	UK Exports as % GNP
		1	2	3	4	5	
1960	24.34						22.56
1961	22.59	(1.75)	1.1	5.15	3.61	(.57)	21.99
1962	21.92	(.67)	1.3	7.00	1.34	(.47)	21.52
1963	21.87	(.05)	(.6)	7.35	4.09	(.16)	21.36
1964	22.88	1.01	.2	10.20	5.29	(.53)	20.83
1965	21.85	(1.03)	1.8	7.9	2.85	.05	20.88
1966	21.56	(.29)	.9	8.7	1.92	.36	21.24
1967	21.99	.43	(.1)	5.95	1.76	(.54)	20.70
1968	24.83	2.84	[−9.6] .4	11.65	2.85	3.08	23.78
1969	24.74	(.09)	.3	11.65	2.08	1.40	25.18
1970	25.45	.71			1.59	.93	26.11

Correlations   *Columns*

1961-69/70 No allowance for devaluation	1 & 2	−.4869
	1 & 3	.6767
	1 & 4	.0823
	1 & 5	.6988
	5 & 2	−.0916
	5 & 3	.7689
	5 & 4	−.2108
1961-69 allowing for devaluation in 1967 by taking 1968 column 2 as − 9.6	1 & 2	−.8648
	5 & 2	−.8378
1961-67	1 & 2	−.6773
	1 & 3	.6092
	1 & 4	.2774
	1 & 5	−.1142
	5 & 2	.2402
	5 & 3	.3804
	5 & 4	−.2322

Sources: 1971 National Income & Expenditure Blue Book
National Accounts of OECD Countries 1953-69

Table III.9B

IMPORT AND EXPORT RATIOS – Goods and Services
Based on 1963 Prices

Year	UK Imports as % GNP-FC	Increase as % GNP-FC UK Imports on Previous Year	Deflator Measure Loss Competitiveness	% Growth all OECD Trade	% Growth UK GNP-FC	Increase as % GNP-FC UK Exports on Previous Year	UK Exports as % GNP
		1	2	3	4	5	
1960	22.78						21.41
1961	21.83	(.95)	1.1	5.15	3.61	(.13)	21.28
1962	21.95	.12	1.3	7.00	1.34	.07	21.35
1963	21.86	(.09)	(.6)	7.35	4.09	.01	21.36
1964	22.75	.89	.2	10.20	5.29	(.27)	21.09
1965	22.35	(.40)	1.8	7.9	2.85	.46	21.55
1966	22.56	.21	.9	8.70	1.92	.53	22.08
1967	23.55	.99	(.1)	5.95	1.76	(.29)	21.79
1968	24.61	1.06	[−9.6] .4	11.65	2.85	2.04	23.83
1969	24.82	.21	.3	11.65	2.08	1.69	25.52
1970	25.87	1.05			1.59	.80	26.32

Correlations   *Columns*

1961-69 or 70 No allowance for devaluation	1 & 2	−.4974
	1 & 3	.5214
	1 & 4	−.1609
	1 & 5	.2744
	5 & 2	.0244
	5 & 3	.7857
	5 & 4	−.2753
1961-69 allowing for devaluation in 1967 by taking 1968 column 2 as − 9.6	1 & 2	−.5521
	5 & 2	−.6611
1961-67	1 & 2	−.5129
	1 & 3	.4576
	1 & 4	−.0370
	1 & 5	−.3773
	5 & 2	.5787
	5 & 3	.2469
	5 & 4	−.3809

Sources: 1971 National Income and Expenditure Blue Book
National Accounts of OECD Countries

Table III.9C

IMPORT AND EXPORT RATIOS – Goods and Services

	Imports		Exports	
	Increase as % UK GNP Imports on Previous Year	UK Imports FC as % GNP-FC	Increase as % UK GNP Exports on Previous Year	UK Exports FC as % GNP-FC

(Current Prices)

	Actual		*Actual*	
1960		24.34		22.56
1961	(1.75)	22.59	(.57)	21.99
1962	(.67)	21.92	(.47)	21.52
1963	(.05)	21.87	(.16)	21.36
1964	1.01	22.88	(.53)	20.83
1965	(1.03)	21.85	.05	20.88
1966	(.29)	21.56	.36	21.24
1967	.43	21.99	(.54)	20.70
1968	2.84	24.83	3.08	23.78
1969	(.09)	24.74	1.40	25.18
1970	.71	25.45	.93	26.11

	New Policy Predictions		*New Policy Predictions*	
1971	3.04	28.49	2.21	28.32
1972	1.08	29.57	1.50	29.82
1973	1.50	31.07	.75	30.57
1974	.39	31.46	.50	31.07
1975	.65	32.11	.25	31.32

	Current Policy Predictions		*Current Policy Predictions*	
1971	.86	26.31	.39	26.50
1972	1.26	27.57	.00	26.50
1973	.32	27.89	.50	27.00
1974	.35	28.24	.50	27.50
1975	.66	28.90	.50	28.00

National Product and the three principal factors influencing these changes. The difference between Table III.9A and III.9B is that Table III.9A is based on current prices while those in III.9B are in 1963 prices. Both tables are included as a check on each other and they show slight variations, though none of great significance. The figures quoted in the text which follows are taken from Table III.9A — i.e. they are based on current prices as are the figures in Table III.9C.

Looking first at the percentages for imports and exports themselves the immediate point which strikes one is how consistent both percentages were up till 1967, particularly in the case of exports. This is not a healthy trend at all bearing in mind that world trade was consistently growing faster than world Gross National Product during the sixties, so that on average every country's exports and imports were growing as a proportion of their Gross National Products. However, after the 1967 devaluation exports rose far more as a percentage of the Gross National Product than in any of the previous seven years, 3.08% in 1968 dropping back to 1.40% in 1969, and dropping again in 1970 to .93%, though even this last figure is a bigger gain than any other before 1968. On the import side the picture is much more erratic with a percentage increase of 2.84% in 1968 followed by a reduction of .09% in 1969 but with a rise of .71% in 1970. Import percentages were rather more erratic than those for exports throughout the period. Of course it is only to be expected that both imports and exports should rise as percentages of the Gross National Product after devaluation, because the prices of both will rise in domestic terms compared to goods not involved with foreign trade for reasons already discussed.

Turning now to the correlations in Tables III.9A, checked by those in Table III.9B, we find that both imports and export percentages are positively correlated with increases in OECD trade, though exports at .7689 rather more so than imports at .6767 (but there is a wider gap between these correlations in Table III.9B). Since increases in world trade were particularly marked in 1968 and 1969, the two years after the last British devaluation, this is a factor to be watched carefully, though the fact that imports as well as exports are positively correlated helps as an offsetting factor. Interestingly there is almost no correlation at all at .0468 between the rate of growth of the economy and the percentage of imports to Gross National Product, but exports are negatively correlated, if rather weakly at .2753. This is again a point of danger tending to suggest that when the British economy is growing production tends to be drawn to the domestic market away from exports. One of the main reasons for the undervaluation policy is to try and counteract this tendency by making exports much more profitable. There is very little correlation indeed at .0161 between changes in import and export percentages, though one suspects that this is more a measure of the random movements of import percentages rather than anything else. Correlations between the deflator measure of competitiveness and import and export percentages are not very reliable because the results obtained depend very much on when the effects of the 1967 devaluation are assumed to begin to affect import and export percentages, and whether it is reasonable to assume that all of a relatively very substantial change can be deemed to have had its effect within one year only, or whether the effects should be spread over a longer period of time. In the table it has been assumed somewhat arbitrarily that all the effect of the 1967 devaluation, which took place in the middle of November 1967, could be taken in 1968. The result is to change a deflator measure of competitiveness for 1968 from 0.4% by 10.0% – an estimate for the overall change in domestic as against external prices in 1968 compared to 1967 – giving a net figure of −9.6%. This is an admittedly unsatisfactory procedure, but for what it is worth it gives a high negative correlation for exports, −.8378, which is what one would expect, but also a high negative correlation for imports at −.8648 which is not what one would expect at all. The equivalent correlations in Table III.9B are of smaller order of magnitude but in the same direction. It might well be supposed that increasing domestic as against foreign prices would lead to a lower proportion of the Gross National Product being devoted to imports but this is not what we find. Since this is an important result a further correlation was done for the period 1961-67 when any result obtained could not have been caused by distortions caused by the devaluation. The result is still a negative figure for imports, at −.6773, but a similar check on the correlation for exports now shows a weaker positive correlation figure for exports, of .2402, which is again precisely opposite to what one would expect. The equivalent figures in Table III.9B confirm the picture even more strongly.

It must be admitted that this is not a very satisfactory lot of evidence to use for making firm predictions about what is going to happen if Britain devalues the pound again. However there is enough consistency and firmness of direction about these results for us to be able to come to at least some definite conclusions. The safest procedure seems to be to regard as acceptable foundations any clear movements in the figures which could be easily predicted from theoretical considerations, and then to consider carefully whether there are likely to be perverse movements by other factors which are likely to upset the policy we are propounding.

On the export side we would both expect and find a definite increase in the proportion of Gross National Product devoted to exports after the 1967 devaluation and we also see a fairly sharp initial increase, falling away as adjustments to the new parity are made. We can therefore safely say that a similar effect is likely to be experienced again with a reasonable substantial devaluation. However, it appears from the positive correlation between rising export percentages and rising U.K. prices compared to overseas, that this effect does not manifest itself when relative price changes are small. This can probably be explained by the fact that small export price increases do not cause export customers to cancel orders or change suppliers but they do, at least for a period of time, lead to more revenue from exports and thus an increase in their percentage of the Gross National Product. It also seems very likely that a similar explanation can be advanced to explain the negative correlation between import percentages and relative reduction in overseas prices, although devaluation did not seem to upset this tendency very much after 1967 in contrast to exports which were evidently considerably affected.

Perhaps it would be helpful at this stage to state the conditions which have got to be fulfilled for an undervaluation policy to work, and check these off against the results found to date:

1. Exporting must become more profitable. This condition will clearly be met.
2. Exports must increase as a proportion of Gross National Product. We are safe in assuming this will happen.
3. There must be at least a tendency for imports to increase more slowly than exports as a percentage of Gross National Product. Evidence for this is not as firm as one would like to see, and the success of the last devaluation has depended heavily on the percentage fall in imports in 1969, which could not have been predicted as a result of anything which happened previously, and which is difficult to account for even after it has shown up in the statistics. Provided something similar to the average results achieved between 1968 and 1970 occurs again with another devaluation there would be nothing to worry about. However,

one rather worrying aspect of Britain's tendency to import, following from the unexpected negative correlations we have found, is that our overall elasticity of demand for imports may be extremely low, implying that roughly the same volume of goods will be bought whatever the price. This may well be a good point for selling a policy of undervaluation to other countries but it does not help to make this policy easier to work from a domestic point of view. The condition to be satisfied for a policy of devaluation to work is that the elasticities of demand for imports and exports together shall be more than unity. If elasticity is very low on the import side, then it has to be that much higher on the export side. Fortunately it appears that this condition is comfortably met provided that the devaluation is fairly substantial, *but not apparently otherwise.*

The conclusion to be drawn from this analysis is that no New Policy is going to work unless it allows for a substantial increase in imports with the main benefit to the balance of payments coming from an even larger increase in exports. In more detail, the New Policy budget assumes that a rather larger devaluation than the last one will produce a slightly smaller increase in exports as a percentage of Gross National Product per annum — 2.0% in the first year, 1.5% in the second, .75% in the third, .5% in the fourth and .25% in the fifth. On the import side imports are treated as a residual balancing item after all the other claims on the output of the economy have been taken off — i.e. National Income minus Domestic Investment minus Exports minus Consumption equals Imports. *Ex post* this equation is or course impeccable; the question is whether imports will have a priority in fact which means that the values in the equation will be upset by balance of payments considerations leading to a sub-optimal size of National Income. To allow for this tendency a further restraint has been imposed upon the budget which is that in no year should the *volume* of imports be allowed to fall as a *percentage* of the volume of the Gross National Product. This condition does meet all the requirements arising out of experience from the last ten years and is therefore one which it is felt makes the New Policy budget proposals viable, and it should be noted that this condition would still allow the New Policy to work without a repetition of the unexplained drop in percentage imports in 1969.

Before leaving the matter of imports and export percentages one point to be covered is this: if it is true that with small relative annual price movements imports tend to fall and exports to rise as sterling costs rise in relation to the rest of the world, what is the point of devaluation? Are not all the benefits being gained without devaluation? The answer is that they will not, and it is easy to see why by looking at Table III.8, particularly for 1964. While it appears that import percentages consistently have a negative correlation with domestic competitiveness, exports only have a positive one in conditions of deflation. Since it is this very condition of deflation which we want to break out of, we cannot rely on this effect to avoid devaluation. In mathematical terms this is shown for the years 1961-67 by the negative correlation of $-.3810$ between growth of export percentage and growth of Gross National Product.

New Policy Budget 2 — 6% Cumulative Growth Per Annum

This discussion of the situation with regard to what one can reasonably anticipate on import and export percentages has been rather lengthy because of the extreme importance to be attached to getting as much as possible out of the available evidence. Having done this we are now in a position to turn back to Table III.8. This table is laid out in two sections. At the top are to be found the predicted values for the main measurements of the output of the economy showing how their different values are built up and related to each other, and at the bottom there is laid out the basis for calculating the output of the economy for the following year. The figures for 1970 are taken from the 1971 *National Income and Expenditure Blue Book*, and all the figures shown throughout the table are at 1970 prices. It should be noted that the entries making up the balance of payments on current account have been split into two. On the one hand there are imports and exports of goods and services, which form the part of our foreign payments which is directly affected by devaluation; on the other hand there is Net Property Income from Abroad which, at constant prices, has been a rather steady figure for the last few years, and which has shown no great change as a result of devaluation or other price movements. It has therefore been assumed that this figure would stay at slightly below its recent average each year. The figures shown for Capital Consumption are worked out on the basis of figures to be found in Table III.10. Inspection of these figures shows that there is very little correlation between Gross Domestic Capital Formation and Capital

Table III.10

UK Capital Consumption 1949-70

	CAPITAL CONSUMPTION			GROSS DOMESTIC CAPITAL FORMATION		
	Capital Con-sumption	Increase on Previous Year	Increase as % Previous Year	Increase as % Previous Year	Increase on Previous Year	GDCF
1949	1395					2497
1950	1446	51	3.65	5.40	135	2632
1951	1493	47	3.25	.37	10	2642
1952	1530	37	2.47	.41	11	2653
1953	1586	56	3.66	10.85	288	2941
1954	1653	67	4.22	8.50	250	3191
1955	1724	71	4.29	5.64	180	3371
1956	1775	51	2.95	4.56	154	3525
1957	1838	63	3.54	5.30	187	3712
1958	1903	65	3.53	.67	25	3737
1959	1974	71	3.73	7.70	288	4025
1960	2058	84	4.25	9.76	393	4418
1961	2144	86	4.17	10.30	429	4847
1962	2222	78	3.63	.37	18	4829
1963	2318	96	4.32	1.71	83	4912
1964	2434	116	5.00	16.55	813	5725
1965	2546	112	4.60	4.10	235	5960
1966	2664	118	4.63	2.55	152	6112
1967	2805	141	5.29	6.74	412	6524
1968	2939	134	4.77	4.99	326	6850
1969	3073	134	4.55	(1.06)	(73)	6777
1970	3213	140	4.55	1.60	109	6886

Source:— *1971 National Income & Expenditure Blue Book* (H.M.S.O.) All Financial Figures in £m.

Consumption, and that the latter is a much steadier figure than the former. In any case, because the proportion of the National Income in the U.K. which has gone to investment has been relatively low recently, it seems reasonable to suppose that a sharp rise in Gross Domestic Capital Formation would not be followed immediately by a particularly large increase in Capital Consumption. This is an area where there is some gain to be had in moving from a low to a high rate of investment.

The assumption made, therefore, is that Capital Consumption would rise at 5% per annum, rather more than the recent average, but not as fast as new investment.

Assuming that the New Policy had been put into effect at the beginning of 1971, we are now in a position to trace through what would happen for the next five years. With a well undervalued currency exports would be extremely profitable, particularly as it should not be necessary to cut prices much in terms of external currencies to get extra business. Every effort should have been made to drive home to British industry the scale of the opportunity in front of it, and to explain that investment could be undertaken safely on the near certain assumption that there would be ample demand to ensure a high utilisation rate from abroad as well as from domestic sources. Experience from 1968 suggests that the response to new export opportunities is fairly rapid, and 1968 also saw the best value for I for any year in the sixties apart from 1964. However, whereas in 1967/8 devaluation was accompanied by deflation, this time no such policy should be pursued. Every effort should be made to keep up the pressure of demand including some increase in domestic demand. The new sheer profitability of the export market would avoid too many goods being sucked on to the home market. The object should be to get the value of R up to 0.4 for the first year of the New Policy, 1971. This is not an unreasonable figure either from British experience in the past when boom conditions have been allowed, especially after a year of deflation, and a larger figure than 0.4 was achieved in 1964 by the British economy. Other countries, particularly Japan, have achieved values of R well in excess of 0.4 for years on end (see Table III.7) and have done so without a deflationary situation, to recover from allowing previously under-utilised resources to boost R up. In the analysis which follows, incidentally, it should be noted that reductions in unemployment of labour are dealt with directly whereas reductions in under-utilisation of capacity are allowed for in exceptionally high values for R while the slack is taken up.

The next step is to ensure that a high proportion of the extra output is deployed into increasing net investment, even if the extra claims put on the output of the economy lead in the first year to a considerable worsening in the balance of payments. The figure shown of a 25% increase in net investment is an estimate of the maximum amount which it would be possible to achieve based on both British and overseas experience; if this figure seems rather high, it should be remembered first that the investment industries in Britain were very slack at the beginning of 1971, and second that a 25% increase in net investment implies a very much smaller percentage increase in gross investment. In fact for 1971 the limiting factor would have been not so much one of physical resources as of the time taken to get new investment projects planned and into execution. However, the sustained large increases in investment planned for subsequent years would involve investment industries themselves gearing up for much larger output. The outcome for 1971 would be a percentage growth in Gross National Product of 5.32% and in consumption of 3.5%.

The next year, 1972 in the budget, would in many ways be the most critical. It would be the year which would involve the most change because it would be the one which started to make a real break with the past as the economy geared up for sustained high growth. Inflationary pressures would be strong. While it might be necessary to put as much of a brake on inflation as possible by appealing to industry not to put prices up and to trade unions not to press for very large wage increases, if a choice had to be made between inflation and deflation then there should be no hesitation in accepting inflation. The situation would have to be judged extremely carefully, and some fiscal curbs on consumption might be necessary if it tended to rise too sharply, i.e. above the 4.0% which could be allowed in 1972, but whatever happened the tendency to fight inflation with deflation must be resisted. The likely total amount of inflation over the whole period 1971-75 resulting from this policy will be discussed later.

Assuming that the pressure of demand could be kept high in 1972 there should be a treble gain during this year. First we could anticipate another very high value for R partly because there would still be some previously under-utilised resources being pressed into use, second the increased amount of investment in the previous year would show a larger return, and third in 1972 we could anticipate a considerable reduction in unemployment. Unfortunately there is about a year's time lag between the implementation of policies to reduce unemployment and their having an effect on the ground. However, even if there was no benefit from this source in 1971, it should show up in 1972 and it is anticipated that the extra output per employee returning to work would be about £1,000 p.a. so that a reduction of 250,000 in the number unemployed would lead to an extra £250m in output without any further capital investment. The conjunction of these three additional sources of output would allow a further 20% increase in net investment, a 4.0% increase in consumption and a temporary improvement in the balance of payments. Since on past performance in this country and elsewhere it is difficult to have values of R sustained at 0.4 for very long, it would be only reasonable and prudent to think that R might well fall back in 1973. This being the case, the surplus on the balance of payments should be kept in reserve for future years when it would certainly be needed rather than used up on increased consumption at this stage. The overall increase in Gross National Product in 1972 would be 6.82%.

1973 shows R falling back to 0.3 but the very substantial increase in investment in the previous two years would allow there to be a further substantial increase in output supplemented by a further contribution of £250m resulting from a further large reduction in unemployment. Thus in 1973 it would be possible to achieve a further 20% increase in net investment, and another 4.0% rise in consumption without the balance of payments running into difficulties. Because of the anticipated reduction in the value of R, the increase in the Gross National Product would fall back slightly to 5.88%. Again this kind of result would only be achieved if demand were held up even at the risk of inflation.

1974 and 1975 would see the much higher levels of investment achieved over the last few years really paying off, even though it is assumed that the value of R stays only at 0.3 despite high demand levels. Increases in the Gross National Product would now settle down at over 6.0% per annum. The main gains from rising I and R would now have been achieved, but to keep on getting nearer to the optimum position with considerably higher values of I still the annual percentage increase in investment — at 10% — should be kept above the annual increase in G.N.P. If this policy were to continue it would be necessary to have slightly smaller increases in consumption than 6.0% p.a. to avoid problems with the balance of payments. However it might be that these predictions are too pessimistic. The Japanese experience suggests that sustained values of R of .35 are possible, in which case I could be raised more rapidly without consumption being reduced. The importance of obtaining the highest possible values of R is thus emphasised yet once more.

The overall result of the New Policy would be to raise I from roughly .135 to over .200 and R from the 1970 value of .1378, or the 1960's average of .1769 to .300 over a five year period. The rise in the value of total benefit adjusted downwards 3% for unemployment in 1970 and 1% in 1975 would be from 14.42 to 20.63 during the five year period without allowing for reductions in the balance of payments surplus which would make the change even more marked. Furthermore the position in 1975 would be sustainable, and indeed there is no reason why from the 1975 platform the British economy should not push ahead to Japanese levels of total benefit. This would certainly be a remarkable turn round, and its very rapidity may make many people wonder whether, after all the years of poor economic performance which we have seen in Britain, such a change is really possible. Perhaps it is worth citing again the case of France in the mid-fifties, where policies not unlike those advocated here were pursued, as an example of what has actually been achieved against an unpromising background by keeping the pressure of demand up most of the time. Nevertheless we must turn back to the main doubts which may remain about the practicability of this New Policy, and in particular we must have another look at the total amount of inflation such a policy is likely to cause, and check on the likelihood of Britain being able to achieve sustained high values of R. We must then look at the implications for our New Policy of Britain joining the Common Market. Finally we must check over the various other links in the chain of argument put forward to see what could go wrong with this New Policy which would defeat its intent.

The New Policy and Inflation

On the subject of inflation we have already calculated that the amount of *extra* inflation generated by a policy of 20% devaluation would be about 6% in the first year, 3% in the second year, and 1½% in the third year. The second inflationary, danger from the New Policy is that running the economy at a high pressure of demand may cause demand inflation on top of the cost inflation already derived from devaluation. On this subject there are a number of points to be made. First, while it is true that the New Policy does depend very much on a high and sustained level of demand, it does not need excess demand to make it work so that a situation of 'overheating' is one which is not particularly likely to come about. This point is reinforced by a second one which is that 'overheating' occurs when there is not enough supply capacity to meet demand; however one of the main objectives of the New Policy is to get the supply capacity there, in the form of increased investment, before excessive demand is imposed upon it. This in itself should help to avoid the 'overheating' type of situation. Third, it is now widely agreed among economists that in so far as it is possible to separate out 'demand pull' and 'cost push' inflation, the latter is the more important influence. This leads on to the final and more general point which relates to the way in which the inflationary spiral works. If wage and salary earners have got used to a certain percentage increase per year and there is very little increase in output each year from the economy, then wage and salary increases in these circumstances are purely inflationary. However, if, instead, there is a substantial increase in output available for consumption each year, then this represents an important dampening influence on the inflationary spiral because it means that at least a proportion of wage and salary increases can be absorbed by rising productivity. It is always dangerous to extrapolate old trends into new situations, but it is also very important to get at least some idea of the order of magnitude of inflation with which we might be involved in the New Policy conditions, so the following should not be taken too literally but only as an indication of what seems most likely.

Table III.11 gives a guide to the trends which we might expect to see over the period 1971-75. For each year four different factors influencing inflationary pressures have been distinguished. The 'Inflationary Base' is a measure of the size of wage increase which can be anticipated on past performance even in a situation where there was no increase in output whatever. It is therefore a measure of institutional inflationary pressures which are not related to whatever conditions happen to obtain in the economy and which are not expected to alter over the period. To this is added a figure for 'Pressure of Demand' which is approximately half the value of the additional 'Consumption Available'; it is anticipated that boom conditions will lead to some additional pressure leading to price rises, partly as a result of increased demand, and partly as a result of more pressure for wage increases in boom conditions. The inflationary impact of devaluation has already been discussed. Finally increased Consumption Available (taken from Tables III.8 and III.14) is treated as a dampening factor to be subtracted from the other inflation-generating influences to give an anticipated annual rate of inflation. What is significant about the figures shown is that while the earlier tendency of the New Policy is to produce a higher rate of inflation than the present policies, after three years (by 1974) the position is reversed. Not too much reliance should be placed upon such tentative guesses as are shown in Table III.11, but

Table III.11

Estimates on Inflation 1971-75

		Policies	
		Current	*New*
1971	Inflationary Base	8%	8%
	Pressure of Demand	1.5%	2%
	Devaluation	–	6%
	Less: Consumption available	(3.0%)	(3.5%)
	Inflation	6.5%	12.5%
1972	Inflationary Base	8%	8%
	Pressure of Demand	2.5%	2%
	Devaluation		3%
	Less: Consumption available	(5%)	(4%)
	Inflation	5.5%	9%
1973	Inflationary Base	8%	8%
	Pressure of Demand	2%	2%
	Devaluation		1.5%
	Less: Consumption available	(3.5%)	(4%)
	Inflation	6.5%	7.5%
1974	Inflationary Base	8%	8%
	Pressure of Demand	1.5%	2.5%
	Devaluation		1%
	Less: Consumption available	(2.5%)	(5.0%)
	Inflation	7.0%	6.5%
1975	Inflationary Base	8%	8%
	Pressure of Demand	1%	3%
	Devaluation		–
	Less: Consumption available	(1.5%)	(6%)
	Inflation	7.5%	5.0%
	Total Inflation over Period 1971-75 straight addition	33.0%	40.5%
	Cumulative	37.6%	47.4%

if the estimates shown are broadly along the right lines it may be that over anything but the shortest period the New Policy is actually less inflationary than those pursued at present, whose record of combining stagnation with inflation certainly compares very unfavourably with the record in other countries. Nevertheless the fact must be faced that the immediate impact of the New Policy will inevitably be to produce more inflation and not less.

This may not seem a very palatable prospect, but it is vital that the inflationary price to be paid should be got into perspective. Our previous investigations of inflation have shown that it is not inflation *per se* which people object to so much, as what they think its consequences will be, and one of the most important points about the New Policy is that it takes nearly all the sting out of the consequences leaving inflation as little more than a problem of the inconvenience of not having prices the same every month. The consequences regarding the balance of payments can be taken care of by floating the pound. The problem of redistribution of income is not insoluble. The effect on maldistribution of investment is quite small and could be made still smaller by better policies. If the price to be paid for an economy growing at 6% per annum instead of 2.5% per annum is a once and for all extra inflation of 10% spread over three years it is submitted that this is a very low price to pay. It should also be borne in mind that not only will the New Policy produce extra growth, it will also rapidly reduce the number of unemployed. Is it really better to have nearly a million unemployed than an extra 10% inflation, quite apart from the question of increased growth?

How to Increase the Social Rate of Return;
The Importance of Investment Gestation Periods

We must now turn to the question of seeing what can be done to ensure that the high values of R posited in the New Policy are attained. We have noted several times already that high values of R are partly a function of keeping up a high level of demand and partly a matter of seeing that investment carried out is of a type which has got a substantial potential contribution to make to R. Policies for keeping up demand have been discussed at length already and the object of this section is to concentrate attention on ensuring that investment is made in the right areas rather than it is used to the full once it is installed.

The correlation which we have already found between high values of I and R and rapid economic growth suggests that rapid economic growth and a high level of investment leads to a more efficient allocation of investment and a more efficient economy generally, in a static sense, than the conditions which apply when growth is slow. The Japanese experience certainly tends to bear this out, and it is not difficult to see why this should be so in terms of economic organisation. When growth is rapid able management can get to the top more quickly than it can in more sluggish conditions. Efficient organisations grow relatively faster than inefficient ones. New techniques are put into practice more rapidly and the average age of capital equipment goes down with cumulatively larger amount of investment each year. Change becomes much more endemic in the fabric of society, and with low unemployment and a rapidly changing environment, restrictive practices become much less of a problem. With more growth there are more resources available for eduction, a slow but vital ingredient in any successful economic mix. All these gains from a rapid growth tend to lead to higher values of R, or, more accurately, of the potential value for R given the right demand conditions. It is also noteworthy that many of the changes which rapid growth brings are ones which many people would welcome on general social grounds as well as on narrower economic ones.

We have also noted already that much of the influence of the government on economic affairs is devoted to what amounts to raising potential R. These policies range from anti-monopoly legislation to bills on industrial relations, from subsidising research and investment to arranging mergers in industry. The analysis developed so far strongly suggests that as methods of improving R these policies are relatively very ineffective compared with increasing the pressure of demand in the short term, and that in the longer term the process of rapid economic growth itself will do a lot more to improve potential R than any amount of government policies devoted to reorganising sections of the economy. However, there is one area in which the government has a very great deal of influence and where substantial changes could be made over quite a short period of time which could make a really noticeable difference to the potential value of R for the economy as a whole. This has to do with the power which the government has, both by subsidies and by direct control, over what investment is undertaken, and the scope for improving values for R lies in improving investment appraisal techniques.

It will be recalled that the assumption made in Chapter II with regard to the gestation period for investment was that this was one year on average. More strictly what was assumed was that consumption foregone in year 0 led to increased output in year 1, so that the average length of time taken between consumption foregone and the benefit from the corresponding investment being received was six months. If the resources devoted to investment — and our measure of investment included stocks and work in progress — were put into it evenly over the period from when the investment started to take shape to the time when it came on stream and started producing, then our assumption was that on average investment started now would come on stream in exactly one year's time. Of course some investment takes much less time than this to mature and other projects takes much longer. In Chapter II we investigated the possibility that if the average period of gestation was not a year but a longer or shorter period, then using standard national income statistics might lend a bias to the values of R thrown up by them. We came to the conclusion then that the possible bias from this source was very small and could be ignored. However at the time we also noted that the contribution made to R by an investment with a long gestation period was much lower than an investment with a shorter one, even if the social rate of return of two projects was the same once they were on stream. This is an extremely important matter which must now be gone into in some detail.

Before getting down to quantification it may help to state the essence of the matter verbally. What investment does is to increase productivity by producing a higher output per unit of input than was available previously. When the higher output is achieved it can be used partly for increasing consumption and partly for undertaking further investment in the future. Now of course it is most important that investment undertaken should lead to as large an increase in productivity as possible, but there is also a further very important point to be added. The shorter the time taken between the sacrifice of consumption which makes available the resources for investment and the time the investment comes on stream, the more often within any given time span the cumulative benefits from investment becomes available to the economy and hence the community.

The significance and importance of this point becomes apparent when it is considered mathematically. There are three paradigm cases to be considered, one being the case of investment where all the sacrifice is made in year 0 (i.e. this year) and the output from it instead of starting in year 1 (i.e. next year), does not become available until some time further ahead. The second case is investment which has a maturity period of less than a year, and the third case is investment which involves annual sums being deployed into it for a number of years before any output is forthcoming from the investment. What we are now concerned to do is to compare the flow of benefit which results from the same quantum of investment with the same social rate of return once it is on stream, but differing in the time taken to produce new output from the moment when resources begin to be deployed into it. We can assess the size of benefit flows in the usual way by discounting the flow of extra consumption into the future allowing for factors D and d. As in the previous chapter the mathematical proofs of what follows will be found in Appendix A to avoid having too much algebra in the text, but the results of quantifying the implications of short and long term gestation periods on the benefit flow from any quantum of investment, with any given social rate of return once it is on stream, are as follows:[18]

General — All benefit flows from particular types of investment are in exact ratio to their social rates of return once their gestation periods have been determined, and the ratio between the benefit flow from investment with any given social rate of return with a one year gestation period and any other gestation period is the reciprocal of the social rate of return that would have been necessary, in the case of investment which has not got a one year gestation period, to make it equal to the benefit flow from the case which had. An example may help to make something which is rather complicated more readily intelligible. Consider the circumstances in Case One below where investment with a two year gestation period is compared with that with a one year gestation period. The ratio between the flows of benefit in this case is $1:D/(1+D)$; the ratio between the social rates of return on the same quantum of investment to produce the same benefit flow in the first case after a one year gestation period and in the second case after two years would be $1:(1+D)/D$.

Case One — Sacrifice of consumption all made during year 0 leads to a quantum of investment which comes on stream not at the beginning of year 1, but at the beginning of year 2, then year 3, and then year n, the general case. The ratios between the size of the flow of benefit from investment with a one year gestation period and the benefit flows from the same quantum of investment with the same social rate of return once it is on stream but with longer gestation periods are as follows:

Gestation Period in Years	Ratio
1	1
2	$\dfrac{D}{(1+D)}$
3	$\dfrac{D^2}{(1+D+D^2)}$
n	$\dfrac{D^{n-1}}{(1+D+D^2+\ldots+D^{n-1})}$

or

$$\frac{(1-D)\cdot D^{n-1}}{(1-D^n)}$$

Values of these expressions for the usual range of values for D, and with n ranging from 1 to 10 are laid out in Table III.12A. Reciprocal values are also shown.

Case Two — Sacrifice of consumption during the early part of year 0 leads to investment whose gestation period is so short that it comes on stream before the end of year 0. In this case the ratio between the size of benefit flow from an investment with a gestation period of less than a year, and one of the same magnitude with the same social rate of return once it is on stream but with a gestation period of one year is as follows:

$$\frac{12}{\text{Gestation Period measured in Months}} : 1$$

In this case it is assumed that we are involved with such a short period between sacrifice of consumption and the investment coming on stream that factor D can be ignored.

Case Three — Sacrifice of consumption at a steady rate for two years, three years and n years, the general case, results in a quantum of investment which comes on stream at the beginning of year 2, year 3 and year n respectively. In these cases the ratios between the size of flow of benefit from investment with a one year gestation period, and the benefit flows from the same quantum of investment with the same

Table III.12A

Ratios between benefit flows for investment where all the sacrifice of consumption is made in year 0 but output does not begin until the beginning of years n values $1 \rightarrow 10$.

$D \rightarrow$	.90	.91	.92	.93	.94	.95	Unweighted Average
n $\downarrow$							
1	1.000	1.000	1.000	1.000	1.000	1.000	1.000
2	.474	.476	.479	.482	.485	.487	.481
3	.299	.302	.306	.309	.313	.316	.308
4	.212	.216	.220	.223	.227	.231	.222
5	.160	.164	.168	.172	.176	.180	.170
6	.126	.130	.134	.138	.142	.146	.136
7	.102	.106	.110	.114	.118	.122	.112
8	.084	.088	.092	.096	.100	.104	.094
9	.070	.074	.078	.082	.086	.090	.080
10	.059	.063	.067	.071	.075	.079	.069

Reciprocal Values

	.90	.91	.92	.93	.94	.95	Unweighted Average
1	1.00	1.00	1.00	1.00	1.00	1.00	1.00
2	2.11	2.10	2.09	2.08	2.06	2.05	2.08
3	3.35	3.31	3.27	3.23	3.20	3.16	3.25
4	4.72	4.63	4.55	4.47	4.40	4.33	4.52
5	6.24	6.09	5.95	5.81	5.68	5.55	5.89
6	7.94	7.69	7.47	7.25	7.04	6.85	7.37
7	9.82	9.46	9.11	8.79	8.49	8.21	8.98
8	11.91	11.39	10.91	10.46	10.03	9.64	10.72
9	14.23	13.52	12.86	12.24	11.68	11.15	12.61
10	16.81	15.85	14.97	14.17	13.42	12.73	14.66

Basis for calculating first table

$$\Sigma B'' = \Sigma B' \frac{D^n - 1}{(1 + D + D^2 + \ldots + D^{n-1})}$$

second table

$$\Sigma B' = \Sigma B'' \frac{(1 + D + D^2 + \ldots + D^{n-1})}{D^{n-1}}$$

Table III.12B

Ratios between the flow of benefit for investment where the input is spread evenly over n years compared with investment with this same social rate of return with a gestation period of one·year — values of n from 1 to 10.

$D \rightarrow$ n $\downarrow$	.90	.91	.92	.93	.94	.95	Unweighted Average
1	1.000	1.000	1.000	1.000	1.000	1.000	1.000
2	.737	.738	.740	.741	.742	.743	.740
3	.591	.593	.595	.597	.599	.601	.596
4	.496	.499	.501	.504	.506	.509	.503
5	.429	.432	.435	.437	.440	.443	.436
6	.378	.381	.384	.387	390	.393	.386
7	.339	.342	.345	.348	.352	.355	.347
8	.307	.310	.314	.317	.320	.323	.315
9	.281	.284	.287	.291	.294	.297	.289
10	.259	.262	.265	.269	.272	.275	.267

Reciprocal Values

	.90	.91	.92	.93	.94	.95	Unweighted Average
1	1.00	1.00	1.00	1.00	1.00	1.00	1.00
2	1.36	1.35	1.35	1.35	1.35	1.34	1.35
3	1.69	1.69	1.68	1.67	1.67	1.66	1.68
4	2.02	2.01	2.00	1.99	1.98	1.97	1.99
5	2.33	2.32	2.30	2.29	2.27	2.26	2.29
6	2.64	2.62	2.60	2.58	2.56	2.54	2.59
7	2.95	2.92	2.90	2.87	2.84	2.82	2.88
8	3.26	3.22	3.19	3.16	3.12	3.09	3.17
9	3.56	3.52	3.48	3.44	3.40	3.36	3.46
10	3.87	3.82	3.77	3.72	3.68	3.63	3.75

Basis for calculating first table

$$\Sigma B'' = \Sigma B' \times \frac{1}{n} \times \frac{(1-D)}{D} \left[\frac{D}{(1-D)} + \frac{D^2}{(1-D^2)} + \ldots + \frac{D^n}{(1-D^n)} \right]$$

Second table is reciprocal of first

social rate of return once it is on stream but with longer gestation periods, are as follows:

Gestation Period in Years	Ratio

$$1 \qquad 1 \text{ or } \frac{1}{1} \cdot \frac{(1-D)}{D} \cdot \frac{D}{(1-D)}$$

$$2 \qquad \frac{1}{2}\frac{(1-D)}{D} \cdot \left(\frac{D}{(1-D)} + \frac{D^2}{(1-D^2)} \right)$$

$$3 \qquad \frac{1}{3}\frac{(1-D)}{D} \cdot \left(\frac{D}{(1-D)} + \frac{D^2}{(1-D^2)} + \frac{D^3}{(1-D^3)} \right)$$

$$n \qquad \frac{1}{n} \cdot \frac{(1-D)}{D} \cdot \left(\frac{D}{(1-D)} + \frac{D^2}{(1-D^2)} + \ldots + \frac{D^n}{(1-D^n)} \right)$$

The values for these expressions, again for the usual range of values for D and with n ranging from 1 to 10, are laid out in Table III.12B. Reciprocal values are shown as well.

The implications of the figures shown in Tables III.12A and III.12B are exceedingly far reaching. It should be noted that the results are relatively insensitive to values of D, so there is very little margin for error in discussing the average values for the expressions given in the final column of each table. These tables show quite clearly that investment with a relatively long gestation period has a very much smaller contribution to make to economic growth than investment with a short gestation period and the same social rate of return once it is on stream. As one would expect, the table for the rather unusual case of investment all made in year 0 with no pay off until years later shows a very rapid fall off in benefit flow, but the fall off is still very marked with the much more typical case of investment which has a long period of gestation with resources being deployed into it year by year in roughly equal amounts. And which are such types of investment? Precisely those which the British government has been most active in fostering during the last few years — atomic energy, computer development and practically the whole of the aerospace industry to take just three examples. To drive home the point let us for a moment consider the Concorde project which in round figures has taken ten years to develop with roughly equal resources being ploughed into it each year throughout the period. This is a clear example falling under Case Three, and Table III.12B shows that the potential social rate of return on Concorde would have to be nearly four times the potential national average for investment with a one year maturity period for this investment to be worth while. Now the changes of the Concorde project ever recovering its production costs, let alone its development costs, are slender, but no-one has ever believed that it was going to produce a social rate of return of nearly four times the potential one year national average rate, yet this is the condition it would have to meet to be justified on the basis of the analysis presented here. Much the same line of argument applied to atomic energy, computers and all the other high technology, research intensive, long pay off industries upon which Britain's future is supposed to lie. The empirical evidence to support the theoretical conclusions reached in this section is plentiful from international comparisons. In so far as one would expect there to be a high correlation between high technology, long pay off industries and the proportion of the national income devoted to research and development, one would expect that countries with a large proportion of the national income devoted to research and development had low values of R. This is exactly what one does find.[19] It is very significant that Japan undertook very little basic research for a long period since the last war and was not much involved with slow pay off industries, most of her industrial success stemming from light industry where technology was copied from other countries. As a result the Japanese value for R was very high. But if one refers back to Table III.7 it can be seen that the Japanese value for R has been falling recently, no doubt because of more concentration on slower paying off investment.

It is submitted here that the reasons normally put forward by commentators on the British economic scene to explain our slow rate of growth, ranging from a reluctance to work hard to the fact that our traditional export markets have been growing slowly, from restrictive practices to lack of salesmanship, are all relatively trivial compared with the two major factors which the analysis in this book has uncovered. The first of these is that because we have had an overvalued currency we have had too little pressure of demand to keep the investment we have undertaken fully utilised, and the second is that we have invested far too much of our nation resources in industries with a very long pay off period — and with mediocre social rates of return in many cases at the end of the gestation period. Proposals for raising the pressure of demand and keeping it up have already been discussed. We must now turn to what policy the government should follow to get the return from investment that is undertaken as high as possible.

Investment Appraisal

Essentially what is required by the government is to change investment appraisal techniques away from private to social rates of return, and to use discounting procedures as in Table III.12 on any investment which is going to take more than a year to come on stream from the time when money starts being spent on it. Social rate of returns may seem to be rather vague, but in fact what they are equivalent to in any particular enterprise is what is normally known as 'value added'. The critical ratio to look for is the ratio between the cost of any investment and the additional value added it is likely to lead to, discounting this value added by the figures in Table III.12. Adjustments to labour inputs can be made using the same sort of procedure as we used in the last chapter. If these techniques were used they would have two major effects. The first is that there would be a substantial movement away from the sort of investment pattern which has been seen in Britain since the last war, where we have tried to stay in the world league in all major high technology development, and in the end we have failed to make the grade in any of them. What we ought to do, at least for the time being, is to use other people's basic research, or buy in advanced equipment if we need it from the United States, Japan and elsewhere, and concentrate on lower technology, and investment which pays off quickly to get our rate of growth up. The other thing which we can do is to look very hard at the time projects take to get on stream. If Table III.12 shows that investment with a very long gestation period is much less valuable than investment with a shorter one, then this is a strong argument for concentrating resources on all investment projects which are undertaken to get them on stream quickly. One of the most dismal consequences of Britain's effort to keep up with everyone else in all high technology industries has been that resources have been relatively thinly spread so that gestation periods are far longer than they are elsewhere. Not only do we lose out in this respect, but also by the time our products do get into use they are getting out of date, so that their value to the economy has already started to fall in relation to competitive products produced elsewhere. This is the story of far too much of British industry during the last twenty-five years. If we are going to stay in any high technology industries we ought to make sure that they are ones where we can keep gestation periods right down, as well as applying the 'value added' yardstick to ensure that they are worth undertaking at all.

However, it should not be thought that this aspect of Welfare Analysis should be applied only to high technology industries. It is equally applicable when investigating, for example, how quickly public works projects such as road building should be completed even if more rapid completion involves some extra costs. Table III.11 shows that the contribution to R of a road which takes two years to build is only about three quarters that of a road which takes one year before it is opened. Nor should it be thought that the general analysis of this book is applicable only to government investment appraisal. The same general techniques can be applied to private investment appraisal, although this is not really a matter for a book primarily involved with economic theory and government policy.

It must be stressed how important it is to improve investment appraisal techniques. We have seen time after time in this analysis that improvements to the value of R are more important in terms of total benefit than anything else, not only because the direct gain to total benefit is substantial, but also because the higher the value of R the more it is worth pushing up I and the easier it is to do so. Furthermore since so much investment is directly or indirectly within the control of the government, this is an area in which major changes in appraisal techniques could be put into effect in quite short order. The submission here is that this would be a far more fruitful field for pressure and direction from the government than many of the areas which have been tackled during the last few years without any great results being achieved.

Welfare Analysis and the Common Market

It will have been noted that in the New Policy five year budget produced and discussed earlier on in this chapter no mention was made of the Common Market. This was a deliberate ommission to make it quite clear that the success or failure of the policy prescriptions put forward were in no way dependent on our joining the E.E.C. However, it is now time to use the analytical tools developed so far to see what light they can throw on the advantages and disadvantages to Britain of joining the Common Market. It must be stressed that since this book is primarily about economics the argument will be confined to discussion of economic matters, and political considerations for or against joining, which must obviously be weighed in the balance, are not included here.

However, it may be apposite to point out first that the vast bulk of the discussion on the Common Market has been on the economic implications rather than any other, and second that economic and political considerations are very difficult to separate out, and therefore if the Common Market is against our economic interests it is most unlikely to be to our political advantage, and *vice versa*.

There is one preliminary point to be covered before getting down to detailed consideration of the implications for total benefit of Britain joining the E.E.C. This concerns the argument that joining the Common Market may not be to our short term advantage, but may well be of benefit to us in the long term. Now in the last chapter a considerable amount of analysis was undertaken into the rate at which it is reasonable to discount the future, and it may be recalled that a rate of less than 5% was regarded as being undemocratic and unrealistic, and one of more than 10% was regarded as being irrationally high. Table III.13 shows the weight, on this analysis, of economic gains achieved in 5, 10, 15 and 20 years' time as against gains achieved this year. Perhaps all that needs to be said is that anyone who propounds economic prescriptions which produce results in ten or fifteen years time at the expense of results before then, is adopting a time preference attitude which we have found exceedingly difficult to accept as having much

---

Table III.13

Discounting Benefit in the Future

Years → D ↓	5	10	15	20
.90	.531	.314	.185	.109
.91	.568	.354	.221	.138
.92	.606	.400	.263	.174
.93	.647	.450	.313	.218
.94	.690	.506	.372	.273
.95	.735	.569	.440	.341
Unweighted Arithmetic Average	.630	.432	.292	.209

Basis for calculation:—

$\Sigma B'' = \Sigma B' \times D^n$

relevance to the real world. Much of the theoretical development in the last chapter was directly concerned with the extent to which it was rational to forego economic benefit now for the sake of extra benefit in the future and there is no doubt at all, if the theory put forward is accepted, that no conceivable benefit in ten or fifteen years time is an adequate substitute for more benefit in the near future. Whatever the gains from joining the E.E.C. may be, they must be in the immediate future to be worth having at all.

The main short term economic advantages for Britain in joining the Common Market must now be examined. These fall under three main headings. First it is argued that a wider market will produce greater specialisation, longer runs and thus general falling unit costs. Second it is suggested that with high technology getting more and more expensive, if Britain is to stay in the world league then she ought to throw in her lot with the E.E.C. countries so that by pooling resources there will be a better chance for everyone to keep up with the Americans and the Japanese. Third it is argued that by associating with the E.E.C. countries, which have grown faster than Britain over the last few years, we will improve our own rate of growth. Let us examine each of these arguments in turn, relating them back to Welfare Analysis criteria to obtain an overall appraisal.

The proposal that a wider market and improved international specialisation involves falling unit costs is one which has an instinctive appeal to it, and it seems certain that some gains will be made from this source. However, various attempts which have been made to quantify these gains have come up with figures which were not very high — 1% in total being about the mark — and not cumulative. In other words during the transitional period there would be a once and for all gain in C of 1%.[20] This is not a negligible amount, but it is not a very large one either — about a sixth of the gain in benefit which could be achieved by reducing unemployment from 1,000,000 to 250,000 for example. Furthermore since the gains in preference we are getting by joining the E.E.C. are more or less exactly offset by losses of preference in the Commonwealth and elsewhere, it may well be the case that the gains in lowering unit costs by joining the Common Market are going to be offset in part or perhaps in full by losses in other directions. The trouble with the E.E.C. is that it is very protectionist, so the net gains from this source do not look very impressive.

The second argument for joining the Common Market is the one which relates to high technology industries. However, our investigations into the contribution which these sorts of industries make to the economies which encourage them was not at all favourable, and if one of the objectives of our joining the E.E.C. is that we should get more involved in this kind of activity than before, then this argument is thoroughly misconceived. Where there definitely could be gains for Europe as a whole would be if each country were to specialise in a particular technology and concentrate its resources into cutting down gestation periods. However there is not much sign of this kind of development at least in the sorts of industries which are not parts of multinational complexes such as I.B.M. It is interesting to contrast the performance of companies such as this which do concentrate their resources on an international scale into rapid and thorough development, and which in consequence are very profitable, with European national companies such as I.C.L. and the French equivalent, Compagnie Internationale pour l'Informatique, which are heavily subsidised and which consistently fail to keep up in getting technologically advanced equipment onto the market quickly enough. In any case, it is far from clear that specialisation in technological developments requires the Common Market to be successful; witness the results achieved by the multinational companies which span many different countries. Nor finally is there any evidence that any mergers or co-operation between companies in different E.E.C. countries is likely to reduce either cost or the gestation periods for investment which they undertake jointly. If the Concorde project is anything to go by, the results are likely to be exactly the opposite — higher costs and more delays.[21] And in any case this type of co-operation or merger can take place again without either country being involved in the same trade bloc, perhaps with special tariff arrangements made for their particular products. In sum, there certainly are gains to be made in Europe by specialisation, but these are not dependent on Britain joining the E.E.C. However, it is a very moot point whether Britain would not be better to get out altogether of as much high technology as possible, rather than to specialise in it, unless other countries really are prepared to co-operate wholeheartedly. Without this co-operation the argument that a large market is required to support high technology collapses too, since several nationally subsidised companies struggling to compete with each other in the E.E.C. are no more likely to be successful than one nationally subsidised company operating with perhaps one international competitor in one country. If the high technology argument for joining the E.E.C. is related to raising potential R, then we must remain very sceptical as to whether it will do so.

We must now turn to what is really by far the most important economic argument for joining the Common Market and see whether doing so is likely to raise Britain's growth rate. It may well be worth while at this stage rehearsing quickly the conditions which we have found to be the most important in achieving this objective. What is required above all is a high pressure of demand generating a high rate of expectation to encourage investment, with the main pull coming in the first instance from exports to avoid a situation where resources get pre-empted into consumption. We have found so far that the only sure way of achieving these conditions is by a rapid float down in the value of the domestic currency, which is likely to cause increased inflation, a necessary price to pay, until satisfactory values of R and I have been obtained, after which the external value of the currency can be allowed to float up again. There are now two questions to be asked. With present policies in operation is joining the Common Market on the terms offered to us likely to produce the growth conditions outlined above? And secondly, if not, will the Common Market help or obstruct the implementation of the New Policy proposed earlier on in this chapter?

As tariffs between Britain and the E.E.C. countries come down there will no doubt be an increase in trade as a result, though as other preferences are being lost elsewhere it is not clear that the net increase in trade will be very large or whether there will be much net increase at all. However, the countries comprising the E.E.C. are essentially high cost food producing countries but competitive on industrial products, whereas our present trading partners, particularly the Commonwealth, tend to be low cost food producers and relatively inefficient at industrial production. In these circumstances it does not seem at all likely that joining the Common Market is going to produce an export led investment boom. We have already seen that the conditions for such a boom are first an increase in profitability of exporting combined with opportunities to export which are sufficiently certain to provide a guarantee that investment which is undertaken will be fully utilised. Of course there will be individual industries for whom these conditions are met by Britain joining the Common Market, but across the board the increased import competition seems likely to cause just as much hanging back from investment for fear of unmanageable competition, as the new export opportunities are likely to encourage it. The general point is that reducing tariff barriers does not necessarily lead to either higher I or R, whereas the under-valuation policy proposed earlier does. Lowering tariff barriers is much more likely to accentuate whatever the present position is than to engineer a change. Regarding the E.E.C., the only condition which would improve the position for Britain would be if the elasticity of demand for E.E.C. imports from the U.K. is higher than for U.K. imports from the E.E.C. No-one, however, has produced any figures to show that such a condition is likely to be fulfilled, and indeed a cursory glance at the pattern of trade between Britain and the Common Market countries would suggest that the opposite was the case.[22]

There are some further reasons for believing that Britain joining the Common Market is not going to improve our prospects for economic growth in the reasonably near future. As is well known a heavy price has been exacted from us at the cost of entry both in terms of contributions to the Common Agricultural Policy and to the Community Budget. Estimates of what these costs are going to be vary, and they depend very much on the exact pattern of development of food prices etc. over the next few years, but at the end of the transitional period they look like being not less than £500m per annum, and perhaps considerably more. Of the sum involved about half is payable across the exchanges and will therefore represent a burden on our balance of payments. This cost of entry will have two effects which are likely to be inimical to growth here. In the first place the payments abroad are a drain on resources at least some of which could be used for investment purposes, and secondly the need to pay a substantial sum across the exchanges is certain to necessitate a more deflationary, or less reflationary policy than would otherwise be possible. The second effect is likely to be the most important because of the very large impact of lack of demand on growth prospects.

The size of the demand threat to our economic prospects from joining the Common Market on the present terms turns to a very considerable extent on what happens to the value of sterling in relation to the value of E.E.C. currencies. In so far that Britain has tended to have a higher rate of domestic inflation than the E.E.C. countries, any attempt to tie the value of sterling to that of the E.E.C. currencies is certain to involve more deflation in the U.K. and any steps in this direction should be resisted for that reason. It is also unfortunate that the E.E.C. countries have a fear of inflation which, particularly in Germany, has led to a series of deflationary policies whose effect on the Germany economy has been totally disproportionate to any conceivable threat to the fabric of society which the very moderate amounts of inflation involved could possibly pose. However understandable this fear of inflation may be in a country which has been through two hyperinflations with the living memory of many of her citizens, there is no doubt about the fact that this attitude is very damaging to the growth prospects of the whole E.E.C. bloc, and indeed the whole trading world, unless everyone else can be insulated from people to think that deflation is preferable to even moderate rates of inflation. This insulation is likely to be more difficult if Britain is within the E.E.C. than outside.

Furthermore, if Britain really ought to be inside the E.E.C. it is exceedingly unfortunate that we did not take part in the formation of the Common Market at the time when the Treaty of Rome was signed in 1958. The position now is that instead of being a founder member of the club we are very much in the position of being a candidate member. We must therefore be on our best behaviour for the next few years, at least until the transitional period is over and we are a full member. These circumstances have put us in a very poor bargaining position as witnessed by the present entry terms. If we continue in this suppliant posture our prospects of avoiding the deflationary policies which look like looming up in the near future by insisting on our being allowed to pursue policies of growth at the cost of inflation and changes to our external payments arrangements do not look very bright.

This leads on to the final point to be made. One of the attitudes which underlies all the arguments put forward in this book is that economic prescriptions which are worth having should have certain characteristics. First they should be directed to clearly defined and quantifiable ends. Second the way the prescriptions proposed are going to achieve these ends should be clearly spelt out with any theorising backed up by support from all the available empirical evidence. Third the margins of error should be carefully investigated so that the likelihood of any policies proposed going wrong are known, and, where possible, ways of getting them back to the rails again should be prepared in advance. Finally policies which have the maximum effect with the minimum of administrative upheaval are greatly to be preferred to those with opposite qualities. The submission here is that Britain's policy of joining the Common Market to solve her economic problems has not been thought out properly when judged by any of these criteria.

Let us now attempt to sum up the advantages and disadvantages of Britain joining the Common Market in terms of the Welfare Analysis developed in the last chapter. There will be some gain from lower tariff barriers between us and the E.E.C., though little if any overall gain because of preferences lost elsewhere. There is an uncertain benefit here which is offset by the certain loss involved by the Common Agricultural Policy and the Community Fund arrangements which definitely exceed any conceivable net gains from switching preferences towards the E.E.C. and away from our existing trading partners. Thus there is no prospect of C rising as a result of our joining the Common Market; it will certainly fall somewhat. We reviewed the prospects for more rational investment allocation in Europe, particularly for high technology industries, and came to the conclusion that if Europe was really determined to stay in the world league there is certainly scope for specialisation which would improve potential R. However, the likelihood of genuine international co-operation, without which such a policy would be wholly useless, does not seem very great, and in any case such co-operation does not require the Common Market to be put into effect. Prospects for potential R rising as a result of Britain joining the E.E.C. do not therefore look good. On the vital question of whether Britain would be likely to enjoy higher levels of demand and less deflation inside the Common Market, all the indications are that there is certain to be more deflation not less for at least the next few years. The argument that it is worth going through a tough period if we are going to emerge better off in 10 or 15 years time, apart from involving a lot of question-begging in itself, was exposed as being an attitude which involved unacceptable views on rational rates of discounting the future. With R being depressed in the coming years, there is no reason to belive that I would rise. Deflation is also certain to cause more unemployment further reducing total benefit. The unhappy conclusion which we therefore arrive at is that every element in the derivation of a value for total benefit is likely to be depressed. There seems to be no good reason at all for believing that total benefit for Britain will improve as a result of our joining the Common Market, at least on present terms and with present policies in operation.

Current Policy Budget — What will happen if we continue Current Policies — Reflation and Deflation

Earlier on in this chapter a five year budget was constructed to show what the effects of the proposed New Policy would be over this time span. By contrast Table III.14 shows what would be likely to happen

Table III.14

1970-1975 BUDGET – PRESENT POLICIES
All Financial Figures in £m at 1970 prices

	1970	1971	1972	1973	1974	1975
GNP-FC	42,819	43,931	46,148	47,758	48,906	49,646
Less: Capital Consumption	4,132	4,339	4,560	4,797	5,051	5,324
NNP-FC	38,687	39,592	41,588	43,961	43,855	44,322
Less: Net Property Income from Abroad	512	500	500	500	500	500
NDP-FC	38,175	39,092	41,088	42,461	43,355	43,822
Made up of						
Net Investment	5,208	5,345	6,238	6,155	5,920	5,762
Exports G & S	11,182	11,642	12,229	12,895	13,449	13,901
Less: Imports G & S	10,898	11,558	12,725	13,322	13,811	14,350
EEC Costs				150	300	450
Consumption	32,683	33,663	35,346	36,583	37,497	38,059
	38,175	39,092	41,088	42,461	43,355	43,822
% Increase Consumption p.a.		3.0	5.0	3.5	2.5	1.5
Balance of Trade		84	(496)	(427)	(362)	(449)
Balance of Payments Current A/C		584	4	73	138	51
Exports as % GNP		26.5%	26.5%	27.0%	27.5%	28.0%
Calculation re Next Year						
Last Year's Investment		5,208	5,345	6,238	6,155	5,920
Estimated Value for R		.2000	.3500	.2000	.1250	.1000
Extra NDP-FC this year from R		1,042	1,871	1,248	769	592
Increase from Extra Employment		(125)	125	125	125	(125)
Last Year's NDP-FC		38,175	39,092	41,088	42,461	43,355
This Year's NDP-FC		39,092	41,088	42,461	43,355	43,822
Add Net Property Inc. from Abroad		500	500	500	500	500
Capital Consumption		4,339	4,560	4,797	5,051	5,324
Total this year's GNP-FC		43,931	46,148	47,758	48,906	49,646
I	.1346	.1350	.1500	.1400	.1350	.1300
R	.1378	.2000	.3500	.2000	.1250	.1000
% Increase GNP		2.60	5.05	3.49	2.40	1.51

over the same five years if policies broadly speaking along the lines of those pursued at present continue over the period. Table III.14 is built up in exactly the same way as Table III.8 and it is extremely important to understand why they show such different states of affairs at the end of so short a period of time as five years. In quantified form these two tables show the difference between a domestic consumption led boom (Table III.14) and an export led investment boom (Table III.8). Let us consider the build up to Table III.14 in detail.

Starting with the external position, the assumption on which this table is built up is that with or without being pegged, the pound would maintain roughly its present parity, and that if the parity fell in relation to the rest of the world then this would only reflect the fact that inflation had been higher in Britain over the period than elsewhere. In other words such devaluation of the pound as there was would keep our export prices in line with those of the rest of the world without any recourse to the policy of deliberate undervaluation advocated earlier in this chapter. This assumption is in line with the most recent pronouncements by Anthony Barber, particularly in his Budget speech in March 1972. On this basis it is assumed that exports would grow slowly as a percentage of the Gross National Product, from 26.5% in 1971 to 28.0% in 1975. The figures in Table III.9 lend support to a trend of this type. As with Table III.8 imports are treated as a residual and again, although *ex post* this procedure is impeccable, *ex ante* there is no particular reason for believing that the demands of the economy as a whole would necessarily be met in the first instance by domestic production and secondly by imports, or rather that there would be enough exports to pay for all our imports with demand at a high level. With the New Policy, undervaluation used the price structure to shift demand towards exports, thus making a policy of deflation, to avoid balance of payments trouble, much less likely. No such happy circumstance can be guaranteed with present policies. It is therefore assumed that the pressure of demand could not be allowed to get too high because of balance of payments restraints.

As with Table III.8, Table III.14 is in two halves. The top half shows the main aggregates for the economy for the years 1970-1975, with the 1970 figures taken from the 1971 National Income and Expenditure Blue Book and those for 1971-1975 being conjectural. Net Property Income from Abroad remains at £500m per annum, and the figures shown for Capital Consumption, following those in Table III.10, are rather lower than those in Table III.8. The values for R and I shown at the bottom of Table III.14 have been chosen with reference to those shown in Table III.2, by picking values for R, and changes in value for I, which correspond with what has happened in the past at different stages of the relation/deflation cycles.

The relationary policies introduced by Anthony Barber during the summer of 1971 are assumed to have the effect of raising consumption in the second half of the year to produce an overall increase in consumption for 1971 of 3%. These reflationary measures would lead to a rather better value for R than in 1970, but not to much improvement in I because there was so much under-utilisation of investment at the beginning of the year that there was little incentive to increase it much at this stage; R would thus come out at .200 and I more or less the same as in 1970 at .135. Again it is assumed that there is a one year time lag between reflationary moves and much influence on unemployment, so that unemployment would continue to rise during 1971, but would fall slowly during the next three years. The balance of payments would show a substantial surplus.

In 1972 it is posited that there would be a further increase in consumption of 5% leading to much fuller utilisation of resources, a considerably higher value of R at .350 and a rise in the value of I to .150. The economy would grow rapidly — an increase in Gross National Product of 5.05% for the year — but the higher pressure of demand would wipe out the balance of payments on current account. Once it became apparent that this was happening further doses of deflation would be prescribed bringing the increase in consumption in 1973 down to 3.5%. However, as can be seen only too clearly from Table III.2, not only would this deflation bring down consumption and improve the balance of payments position; it would also bring down R and I. Furthermore, by 1973 the costs of joining the Common Market would begin to be felt. In terms of total resource cost a bottom figure seems to be about £500m per annum by the end of the transitional period and £1000m a top figure, all at 1970 prices.[23] A middle figure of £750m per annum has been used in Table III.14 and it has been assumed that this rises by £150m per annum cumulatively during the transitional period. Since about half this real resource cost would have to be paid across the exchanges, it would be bound to add to the deflationary pressures. In consequence values for R and I would fall back during 1974 and 1975 as would rises in consumption. It should also be noticed that no resources are being used in Table III.14 to build up a balance of payments surplus; indeed it is assumed that the balance of payments on current account would only barely be kept in surplus at all. Considering the E.E.C. arrangements for transfer of capital, it might well be that a surplus of this size would be insufficient particularly if a stagnant Britain becomes an unattractive place in which to invest, so that not only would capital exports be inclined to rise, but capital imports would probably be sluggish.

Would these problems cure themselves by the value of sterling being allowed to drift downwards slowly or by a small devaluation to make up for excess inflation here, so that the conditions advocated earlier occurred at least in part by accident rather than by design? It would be comforting if it were probable, but unfortunately there are several good reasons which make this an unlikely occurrence. In the first place we have seen that one of the most important conditions for the success of the New Policy was that exporting should be made very profitable and a guarantee should be given to industry that this state of affairs would continue. This means a conscious policy of undervaluation which would need to be adhered to for a considerable period. This is a totally different situation from one brought about by a small devaluation or a drift down in the value of the pound, which might well drift back up again, giving no-one a guarantee of profitable use of investment. Secondly, in the present climate of opinion the government is likely to oppose too much of a fall in the value of the pound on the grounds that rising import prices are inflationary; furthermore we are going to be under a great deal of pressure from the E.E.C. not to allow the value of sterling to fall — not least because of the fact that the costs of Common Market membership are effectively fixed in E.E.C. currencies, not sterling, so that as the pound falls the cost of joining the Common Market rises. If the consequence of these pressures is only a small downward movement in the value of sterling, we are likely to get the worst of all worlds. The negative correlation between import percentages and the deflator measure of competitiveness, combined with the positive one for exports, during the period 1961-67, suggest that for small changes in the external value of sterling the elasticity effects on the balance of payments may well be perverse, so that a small fall in the parity of sterling is likely to make the balance of payments situation worse and not better, thus piling on the pressures for deflation rather than making them less substantial.

The differences in the circumstances of the economy are so marked in Tables III.8 and III.14, especially at the end of the period, that it is worth summarising again the explanations advanced here as to why this should be so. Essentially there are two reasons. What the New Policy does, which present policies do not do, can be summarised as follows:

1. Using exports as a primer it leads to a situation where the resources needed to move towards a much higher rate of growth are created first and can thus be used for investment·rather than being pre-empted at this stage into consumption.

2. The undervaluation policy advocated not only gets the growth process going but it also enables a much higher level of domestic demand to be maintained without balance of payments difficulties intervening, so that the full benefits of all the investment made are available during the whole of the period when the movement towards rapid growth is being made. It also cuts down unemployment and thus ensures that the fullest possible use is made of the manpower and existing capital resources in the economy.

If these macro-economic policies are supplemented by the use of more efficient investment appraisal techniques so that the value of potential R can be stepped up still further, so much the better.

It need hardly be stated that if the analysis advanced so far is accepted, then Britain's policy with regard to the E.E.C. ought to be radically altered. If the main objective of our joining the Common Market is to improve our economic performance — and if it does not do that it is difficult to see that we are going to be any better off politically — then this policy is very seriously misconceived. If we want to run our economic affairs better, there are ways of doing this which are far more likely to work than joining a trade bloc even on neutral terms. But the terms on which we are joining are very far from neutral; they are going to cost us at least £500m p.a. once the transitional period is over, half in foreign currency, and perhaps considerably more. Furthermore there is a very great danger that all the administrative upheaval involved in joining the E.E.C. is going to distract attention away from what the real problems are, and to put us under a great deal of pressure to pursue domestic policies which are wholly inimical to our best interests, or those of the rest of the world. However, rightly or wrongly we are in the throes of negotiating our way into the Common Market. What should our policy be?

There are two essential battles to be fought. First we have paid far too high a price for the doubtful gains from membership of the E.E.C. and we should insist on this price being reduced. Since everything that the Common Market is supposed to be offering us in terms of increased economic opportunities can be obtained much more simply in other ways, there is nothing to be said for paying more than a notional entry price. Secondly, in no circumstances must the Common Market be allowed to constrain us from taking whatever steps are in our best interests to promote our own economic growth, subject to the very important proviso that we should never pursue a beggar-my-neighbour policy of making ourselves better off at the expense of making other people worse off, though the New Policy proposals at no stage involve any such thing. In particular we would be absolutely wrong either to get involved with any policies which tie the value of sterling to any other currency, or to have anything to do with policies which either directly or by implication make deflation necessary, even if the price to be paid is more inflation. If all these conditions are not met then there is no doubt about the fact that if the analysis put forward in this book is accepted we would be better to withdraw from the Common Market altogether.

The New Policy — What could go wrong?

Before concluding this chapter we must turn back to the New Policy proposals put forward and look carefully again at all the weaker points in the chain of argument put forward to see where the dangers lie to the policy not working so that we can assess what may go wrong, and what we could then do about the situation. Let us take these various points in the order in which they arose.

The first danger to the New Policy is that as it depends on having an undervalued currency, the process of devaluation, even if this achieved by a float down, may cause retaliation on a sufficiently large scale to undermine the principle foundation upon which the policy is built. This is a risk which we would have to take, and the size of the risk would depend very much on our success in explaining to the rest of the world what we were doing and why. In particular we should explain that we do not intend to alter our export prices very much and upset other peoples' markets, and that we also anticipate our being a much better customer for the rest of the world's exports. A comparison between the value of imports shown in 1975 in Table III.8 and III.14 makes this point clear even allowing for the different external value of sterling posited — about 20% lower in Table III.8. Britain is not a very large country nowadays in terms of world trade and the chance of competitive devaluations breaking out everywhere because of action taken by us does not seem to be any more likely in the early 1970's than it was in 1967.

The second possible point at which the New Policy may fail is that undervaluation may not cause an export led boom, However, neither logic nor a mass of evidence both from this country and elsewhere suggests that the policy is likely to fail in this respect. What may happen is that the boom will take longer to get under way than one would hope. In the meantime one would be left with the inflationary consequences of undervaluation which would not be a popular position to be in politically. However, the certain ultimate success of the policy would have to make a waiting period bearable. Again clear explanation of what was going on would help to ensure that the desired results were achieved quickly.

Thirdly, is there a danger that once the boom does start there will be such pressures for wage and salary increases that the resources which should be going to investment get pulled into consumption? This is a danger which could be fairly easily overcome partly by fiscal measures to restrain an excess of consumption, and partly by using inflation, if necessary, to mulct back resources from consumption to investment. It would obviously be a very great help if both management and the trade unions could agree to price and wage restraint during this period so that inflation could be kept as low as possible, but the New Policy would work with no incomes policy in operation at all if necessary. The price to be paid for this luxury would certainly be more inflation, though, as we have seen, there are worse things in the world than that.

Finally, it must be stated that the conditions at the beginning of 1971 were very favourable to the implementation of the New Policy proposals because there was so much slack in the economy at that time that it would have been easy to use the under-utilised resources in the economy, both labour and investment, to create the extra output necessary to get the investment boom growing. What would happen if the New Policy were put into effect, say, at the beginning of 1973 with the conditions in the economy being those shown in Table III.13 at this time? The answer is that the New Policy would still work but it would be necessary to hold consumption back more strongly while it got started, though this would be happening anyway, probably to an even greater extent with present policies, so there would be no net loss even in the short term. However, there would still be considerable scope, even at the beginning of 1973, for using resources in the economy more fully, increasing R and reducing unemployment. However, the fact must be faced that superimposing an export and investment boom on top of a fairly high level of consumption demand would almost certainly lead to a more serious amount of inflation than it would have done at the beginning of 1971. Again turning back to the Welfare Analysis of the last chapter, we must ask the question – is it really better to have very little growth and a high rate of unemployment than it is to have a high rate of inflation, assuming as always that the effects of inflation can be confined to being little more than the inconvenience of having prices altering?

Part 4   Conclusion

The New Policy – What we could achieve

This chapter concludes with a brief statement of the gains to be achieved by implementing the New Policy proposals as against continuing with the policies currently in force, using the yardstick developed in the last chapter. From the figures shown in Table III.8 it can be calculated that the value of total benefit for 1975 would be 20.63, and for the whole of the five year period from 1971 to 1975 it would be 20.83. The explanation for the high value for the whole period compared with 1975 is provided by the substantial gains in benefit to be achieved when recovering from very deflationary conditions. The value of I for the period 1971/75 would be .1957 and the value for R .3299 if we were to achieve the budget figures in Table III.8. However, if our economic future were to take the form shown in Table III.14, the value for total benefit for 1975 would be 13.76, admittedly a very poor figure since 1975 would be an exceptionally bad year, but the value of total benefit for the whole of the five year period from 1971 to 1975 would be only 15.75, hardly better than the average for the 1960's. I for the whole period would be .1379 and R .1913. For those who would prefer a simpler and more familiar measurement, comparison between Table III.8 and III.14 shows that the New Policy proposals should produce a total Gross National Product 15.7% higher in 1975 than current policy starting from the same basis only five years previously.

If the average value for total benefit for all OECD countries continued at the level attained in the years covered by the figures in Table III.4 when it was 17.80 — a situation which will not be achieved if the present world tendency towards deflationary policies continues — then the index number measure of Britain's New Policy five year value for total benefit would be 117, and with present policies continuing it would be 88, a total variation round the OECD mean of 29%. There is no good reason why this higher figure could not be achieved, and every reason to believe that the lower figure will be unless something is done to put better policies into operation. It would also reduce unemployment to 1% or less and get rid of balance of payments problems. It might, too, lead to less inflation.

Chapter IV Reflections on Some of the Political and Social Consequences of Faster Growth

The last three chapters have been concerned specifically with economic matters. However, economics is not a subject which can be dealt with in isolation, and this chapter is concerned with considering some of the wider implications of the policy proposals put forward. In particular it is concerned with some of the political and social consequences of the much more rapid rate of economic growth which should result from the prescriptions proposed. It is also concerned with examining again the attitudes which have allowed so little to be done to put our economic house in order for so long.

Economics and Policy

We have been falling behind steadily now in the economic race for a hundred years. In 1870 Britain had the highest Gross National Product per head in the world; now, if we do not do something to change the situation, we are likely to be overtaken by Spain and Greece within a decade or two, countries which within living memory were plunged in depths of poverty unknown in Britain since the early days of the nineteenth century. Why have we let this happen to us? What has gone wrong with our sense of priorities that we have allowed a dismal failure in the amanagement of our economy to cause us to be short of resources for almost everything, from not paying old people adequate pensions to not supporting the arts properly? The fashionable answer is to say that we have been trying to do too much with too meagre resources and there is no doubt that this is part of the answer. However, this cannot be the whole explanation, since there have been many periods during the last hundred years when resources have been lying idle — not only in the 1930's, but much more recently too. There is something utterly absurd about complaining that we are short of resources when our investment industries are lying idle, when we have a million unemployed, and when we have graduates upon whose education large sums of money have been spent who leave university and cannot get a job.

What seems to have been lacking more than anything else has been an adequate method of ranking and weighting priorities so that there is a rational policy for achieving all, or at least as many as possible, of the objectives which are considered worth aiming for. Of course a great deal of this book has been involved with producing a scheme for getting priorities in the right order with suitable weights attached, but there is more to it than that. Underlying the approach adopted here, both in the sections to do with growth theory and in those involving practical prescription, there has been a certain methodology in dealing with problems which might bear explicit statement. In the first place it involves a belief in the capacity of man to shape his environment as he wants it. If one believes that to a large extent the future is in the hands of fate with inexorable forces pushing not only individuals but whole nations in particular directions, then the scope for altering either one's individual destiny or that of the community as a whole is very limited. If, on the contrary, one believes that ideas are what really count in the last analysis, and that by producing ways of applying them new forces can be produced more potent that the old, then the scope for taking charge of destiny is much increased. Given an attitude of mind which believes that the problems under scrutiny are soluble, the next step in dealing with situations involving several objectives, all of which in some degree conflict with each other, is to work out some maximand or objective which subsumes all the others. Unless this is done it is simply impossible to work out any rational priorities. Following from this it is essential to quantify the weights to be given to all the objectives with which one is involved, so that the problems become amenable to mathematical treatment for finding the optimum combination among the available choices. Once this has been done and the priorities have been settled, one is left with the practical problems of achieving them, and here again there are certain ground rules which are much more likely to lead to successful results if they are followed. The first is to check and recheck the chain of logic underlying any prescriptions put forward to ensure that it is consistent and without gaps, and that at every point where empirical evidence is available it is used to confirm or refute theoretical conclusions. In this way the danger of mistakes in prescription can be kept down to a minimum, but economics is not an exact science and no plan put forward is going to work faultlessly. It is therefore especially important that at all stages the margin for error should be borne in mind, and that plans should be prepared in advance for taking corrective action at any stage if things do not work out as expected. Finally, if one is concerned with achieving results there is everything to be said for policies which involve the minimum of administrative upheavals. As has already been pointed out earlier, major administrative changes soak up energy and other resources as well as taking up a lot of time, and generally distract attention away from problems rather than aiding their solution.

There is nothing very new about any of this methodology. The problem in Britain is that it has simply not been used. One only needs to consider the tone of the debate in this country over the last few years on the Common Market to see that this is so, particularly among those who have advocated that we should go in. What are the real reasons for us wanting to become a member of the E.E.C.? What are the priorities among the objectives supposed to be achieved by our joining, and what weight should be attached to each of them? Which of them really depend on us being inside the Common Market? What is the cost of staying out as against going in? Of the objectives which are supposed to be achieved by our joining, what is the chain of logic leading from our joining the E.E.C. to these objectives being attained? In particular, why do those who think that we are likely to have greater economic growth inside the Common Market than outside think that this is likely to happen? What do they think are the principle causes of economic growth, and why do they think that these are more likely to be there with Britain inside the Common Market than outside? In the discussion which has gone on on all these questions it is a lamentable fact that in far too many cases bald assertion has taken the place of logical analysis.

Far too many of the arguments have been of a kind where resort to empirical evidence has been impossible because it is precluded by the terms in which the arguments are couched. If one person says that Britain ought to be in the Common Market because we are close to Continental Europe, and another says that we ought to stay out because we are an island and therefore separated from Continental Europe, what possible appeal to fact is there to settle this matter? And what has any of this sort of assertion got to do with the advantages or disadvantages of joining the Common Market? It is also incredible to see the lack if quantification of the gains and losses to be had from joining the E.E.C. both in the press and White Paper. If the benefits cannot be assessed or if they are very marginal, how do we know they are going to be there at all?[1] If it is true that more economic growth in the long term is going to offset the heavy cost of joining, by what yardstick do they measure off the cost against the benefit? Since adherents to the Common Market have great difficulty in explaining exactly how the supposed gains are going to be achieved, it is of course quite impossible to discuss the possible margins of error which might be involved since there is nothing from which to measure any errors.[2] Finally the cost of joining in terms of administrative reorganisation is absolutely enormous. It really is appalling that such a major step could be contemplated on such ill thought out premises. So much more could be achieved if the same resources were allocated rationally along the lines suggested in this book.

Faster Growth and Britain's Position in the World

It is fashionable to contrast success in the physical sciences with failure in the social sciences, and to point to the failure of man to order his social and political affairs as efficiently as the scientist or engineer can use the results of scientific discovery in practical applications. Even if part of the explanation lies in the more nebulous nature of the social sciences, and the difficulty of carrying out controlled experiments, this still leaves a good deal of explaining to be done. In Britain, at least as far as economics is concerned, a major part of the problem seems to lie in an unwillingness to use techniques of analysis which are capable of producing reasonable results. Controlled experiments are irrelevant if the right questions are not being asked.[3] The need to identify accurately correct priorities in the domain of economics and to find policies which will work to put them into effect is at least as important as technical advance, for without the first the second cannot be exploited. Certainly one of the results which emerges from the analysis in this book is that technical advance by itself is no substitute for competent economic management in improving the lot of humanity.

This leads on to consideration of the results of our economic failures on our political position in the world. There is no doubt that since our economic prowess began to be eroded about a hundred years ago so our power and influence in the world had declined, and we have become more and more a nation which reacts to events in the world rather than making them happen. We have fought a long rearguard action to preserve what we could of the position we had a hundred years ago, but always by extending the resources we had available rather than creating sufficient new ones, and thus our position has got weaker and weaker. There are few people who would like to see a return to Britain's late nineteenth century role of world policeman, but there are many more who have more reasonable fears that failure on the economic front is going to discredit some of the more worthwhile things which we may be able to offer the rest of the world such as an example of a tolerant but reasonably efficient democratic system, a tradition of freedom and fair play which has not degenerated into licence, and an industrial society which still has a high degree of social cohesion. It is sometimes suggested that these very qualities are responsible for our poor economic performance, but the analysis in these pages has not uncovered one jot of evidence for this contention. Economic failure is neither caused by, nor is a threat to, our social heritage; rather the reverse. Furthermore, not one proposal in this book involves any infringement of this heritage, nor is it in any way impossible for all the New Policy proposals to be put into effect in an entirely democratic manner through existing political institutions.

A further comment to be made relates to applying the analysis developed in Chapter II not only to Britain *vis à vis* the rest of the Western world, but also in a wider sense when the whole of the Western world is considered *vis à vis* the socialist countries. The implications of this analysis clearly pointed to the fact that if a choice has to be made, then to a much greater extent than is normally appreciated inflation is to be preferred to deflation; yet at the present time the Western world is in grave danger of deflating itself into a recession because of fear of inflation. It may also be the case, as we saw on page 70 that in fact it is deflation itself which may be the biggest engine of inflation by one remove — because once people have got used to a rising standard of living then they will demand money increases every year which are not necessarily inflationary, if new output is there to meet them, but which cannot be anything but inflationary when output is stagnant — the very situation which deflation brings about. The irrationality of pursuing deflation to get rid of inflation is thus doubled; not only is deflation an appallingly costly process in itself but it may well make worse the very disease it is supposed to cure. The significance of this situation as regards the socialist countries is that, although most Western economists would regard them as very inefficient in a static sense, static considerations are by no means always the most relevant. Where the socialist countries do score heavily is precisely in the one area which this book suggests is of most vital importance; they continually run with a high pressure of demand, and very rarely is there any situation comparable to a Western deflation. Thus the investment they carry out does tend to be fully utilised, even if it is perhaps poorly allocated and relatively inefficient. In the notation used earlier, potential R for socialist countries may be lower than it is in the West but actual R could still be higher because of fuller utilisation. If I is high as well the conditions for rapid growth are there despite the inefficiency denounced from the West. If the socialist countries do grow faster than those in the West, what of the long term balance of power in the world? Deflation and recession need not happen if rational policies are pursued, but they may well engulf us if we do not order our economic affairs in the whole Western world better than at the moment.

The Social Advantages of Faster Growth

However, it should certainly not be thought that all the gains from a better economic performance would be external; many of them, and perhaps the most important, would be within Britain itself and it is worth spelling out at least what the most important of them would be.

In the first place higher pressure of demand will do more for the less advantageously placed regions of this country than any amount of subsidies in one form or another. What is true internationally is true domestically: trade is better than aid. The same factors will also reduce unemployment down to the lowest possible level which, on international experience, is less than 1% of the labour force, a much lower level than we have ever managed to achieve here for any length of time, and a standard from which we have departed to a grievous extent over the last few years. Furthermore it is difficult to believe that some of the industrial tragedies which have occurred recently would have happened under the New Policy proposals. In particular neither the collapse of Rolls Royce, nor the failure of Upper Clyde Shipyards need have taken place. Of course, an undervalued exchange rate is no substitute for proper financial control and a high standard of management generally, but at least it does give export industries such as these two rather longer to get themselves reorganised without getting squeezed between rising domestic costs and pegged export prices.

Secondly it is wrong to think of a rapidly rising standard of living is just a matter of more consumer durables and better holidays, although there are very few people in fact who do not enjoy these private aspects of affluence. As the national income rises so more resources become available for the social services, and it is a sad fact that the British social services no longer lead the world as they once did, and again this is no doubt because of our slow rate of growth. Faster growth will mean that as well as enjoying more private consumption we will also be able to make much more rapid improvements in the standards of our housing, we will be able to pay our old people decent pensions, and we will be able to bring the National Health Service back to a point where it can bear all the loads which are imposed upon it, to cite only three examples. We will also have the resources to look after our environment properly and we have got to make sure that we do so. Perhaps most important of all we shall be able to devote more and more resources to education which, as we saw earlier on, is one of the most worthwhile of all uses of the national income. Here our record is quite good compared with most O.E.C.D. countries, though we are a very long way indeed behind the standards which prevail in the United States.

More rapid growth will also help another problem which has steadily become more acute and divisive in Britain over the last few years. As a consequence of our slow rate of growth, expectations as to what the social services should provide have grown more rapidly than the national income,[4] and this has caused very considerable strains to arise. As more and more demands are placed on the social services one of three unpalatable alternatives has to be faced. Either the increased demands are met *in toto* in which case further rises in taxation have to take place to meet them, or the demands are met on a first-come-first-served basis in which case suffering and resentment is the consequence, or thirdly attempts are made to administer the benefits of the social services on a means tested basis. Means tests have had a very bad name since the thirties and there is an emotional reaction among those who are subjected to them, but in fact there are also very substantial practical objections to means tests. They are expensive to administer; they put off people from claiming what they are entitled to, and in many cases it is those most in need who are most reluctant to come forward; they involve invasions of personal privacy which are bad in themselves, and finally too many means tested benefits on top of taxation produce a situation where working people are effectively taxed on their marginal income at very high rates providing a marked disincentive work harder. One of the benefits of a much faster rate of growth may be that this problem will be bypassed at least to some extent by making the provision of resources to the social services a much easier business, since the total resources will be increasing at a much more rapid rate.

This leads on to the question of the distribution of wealth and income within British society. This is a problem which, as mentioned earlier, is going to become more acute as the national income starts to rise more rapidly, at least as far as the distributions of wealth is concerned. There is little doubt that the first effect of the New Policy would be to make the rich very much richer, but just as rapid growth tends to make this problem worse, so it may make a solution easier. Firstly, as well as making the rich richer it will also make everyone else better off, and if American experience is anything to go by, what is likely to result is a society where a much larger number of people have a substantial amount of real assets, generally in the form of consumer durables and a house which they own, even if it is on a mortgage. In the United States more than two thirds of the households are in owner occupation compared with about 50% in the United Kingdom.[5] This is a development which should surely be welcomed by everyone. However, this still leaves the problem of wealth distribution untouched at the top end of the scale, and particularly in view of the existing very glaring disparity of wealth, there is an overwhelming case for wealth taxation on a much more substantial scale than exists at present. Most of the rational arguments against wealth taxes turn on disincentive effects, which apply to almost all forms of taxation, and to threats of flight of capital overseas. Both these objections can be largely met by making the wealth tax take the form of a gifts tax payable either at death or at the date of transfer *inter vivos*. Practically every other country in the world has more effective wealth taxes than Britain, so that technical problems cannot be insoluble. The main point is to ensure that the additional wealth created by a high growth policy should be spread throughout the population as evenly as possible.

As regards the distribution of income, or more specifically of consumption, there is not much reason to believe that this will alter very much as the national income starts to rise more rapidly. Discussion of the incidence and scale of taxation in detail is rather outside the scope of this book, although, as we remarked earlier on, the most even possible distribution of consumption follows as a consequence of the views which it seemed most rational to take about the marginal utility of income, subject to the practical restraints put upon such a policy by the problems of disincentives and the need for saving. However, as was suggested a little earlier, one of the most effective ways of ensuring that after taxation and transfer payments the distribution of income is kept within a reasonable balance, especially at the bottom end of the scale, is to ensure that the social services are kept in good repair with easy access to their facilities for everyone. It is a remarkable fact that the total effect of the taxation system in Britain, net of all payments and receipts, is to leave everyone from roughly the twentieth to the ninety-fifth percentile where they were, with the only really substantial transfer of income being made from the top 5% of income earners to the bottom 20%. In so far that it is the social services which are the agency by which these transfers are made effective, their importance as a vehicle for ensuring that income distribution is kept as even as possible cannot be overstressed.

Conclusion

Finally, let us try to get the impact of the New Policy proposals in this book into perspective. Perhaps the first point to make is that they are not going to bring in a new millenium. Indeed in many cases the first consequences of a more rapid growth — higher risks of pollution, more congestions, etc. — may not be desirable, so that improving our economic policy is not necessarily going to solve any of our political and social problems, though it will certainly provide us with more resources for doing so and widen our range of choices. What is still needed is the political and social will to ensure that these new resources are used properly. However, what the New Policy proposed does do is not only to show how to improve our economic performance, but also to provide a yardstick for a global measurement of the extent to which improvements have been made. On the figures produced in Chapter III, over a five year period we can bring our performance from being some 12% below the recent average of all O.E.C.D. countries to 17% above it. In more familiar language, we could within five years increase our growth rate to 6% p.a. every year, cut unemployment to less than 1%, get rid of balance of payments problems and, with a bit of luck, we would have less inflation too. This in itself would be no mean achievement. What it would also do would be to bring Britain back into the main stream of one of the most important things which is ever going to happen to man, the transformation of his material circumstances by intelligent use of the fruits of technology, a process which can only take place with any speed if the economic environment is managed correctly. We have been in a backwater in this respect for too long and it is high time we moved out into the main stream again.

Appendix

Appendix A

1. Proof that the sum of the series

$$C$$
$$C(1 + IR)D$$
$$C(1 + IR)^2 D^2$$
$$\ldots\ldots\ldots\ldots$$
$$C(1 + IR)^n D^n$$

$$= \frac{C}{1 - (1 + IR)D} \quad \text{as } n \text{ tends to infinity}$$

Let $(1 + IR)D = x$

The series can then be rewritten as $C, Cx, Cx^2 + \ldots + Cx^n$

Let the sum of this series equal A

Then $A = C + Cx + Cx^2 + \ldots + Cx^n$

and $Ax = \quad Cx + Cx^2 + \ldots : + Cx^n + Cx^{n-1}$

$\therefore A(1 - x) = C - Cx^{n+1}$

Now as n tends to infinity Cx^{n+1} tends to 0 provided x is less than unity, in which case

$$A = \frac{C}{(1 - x)}$$

Substituting back the sum of the series we are looking for is

$$\frac{C}{1 - (1 + IR)D}$$

However if the value of x, or $(1 + IR)D$ is more than unity each term in the series is larger than the last and the series sums to infinity.

2. Proof that the sum of the series

$$C$$

$$CD + CIRD$$

$$CD^2 + 2CIRD^2$$

$$CD^n + nCIRD$$

$$= \frac{C}{(1-D)} + \frac{CIRD}{(1-D)^2} \text{ as } n \text{ tends to infinity}$$

The series to be summed needs to be split into two. The sum of the first terms — all of which are necessarily less than unity — *viz* C, CD, $CD^2 \ldots CD^n$ is found by the method in Proof 1 above and does not need repeating.

The sum of the second terms $CIRD$, $2CIRD^2 + \ldots + nCIRD^n$

$$= CIR(D + 2D^2 + \ldots + nD^n)$$

Let $A = D + 2D^2 + \ldots + nD^n$ and let us now subtract from A the terms of the series $A(2D - D^2)$

The difference between these two series is now as follows

$$A = D + 2D^2 + 3D^3 + 4D^4 + \ldots + nD^n$$
$$-A(2D - D^2) = -2D^2 - 4D^3 - 6D^4 - \ldots - 2(n-1)D^n - 2nD^{n+1}$$
$$+ D^3 + 2D^4 +$$
$$+ (n-2)D^n + (n-1)D^{n+1} + nD^{n+2}$$
$$\therefore A(1 - 2D + D^2) = D + 0 + 0 + \ldots + 0 - (n+1)D^{n+1} + nD^{n+2}$$

As D is always less than unity so as n rises to infinity the last two terms tend to zero

$$\therefore A(1 - 2D + D^2) = A(1 - D)^2 = D$$

$$A = \frac{D}{(1-D)^2}$$

$\therefore$ The sum of the second terms $= CIR \dfrac{D}{(1-D)^2}$

$$= \frac{CIRD}{(1-D)^2}$$

and the sum of both sets of terms together is

$$\frac{C}{(1-D)} + \frac{CIRD}{(1-D)^2}$$

3. Proof that the sum of the series

$$C$$

$$CD$$

$$CD^2 + CIRD^2$$

$$CD^3 + CIRD^3$$

$$CD^4 + 2CIRD^4$$

$$CD^5 + 2CIRD^5$$

$$CD^6 + 3CIRD^6$$

$$CD^n + \frac{n}{2}CIRD^n$$

$$= \frac{C}{(1 - D)} + \frac{D^2 CIRD(1 + D)}{(1 - D^2)^2}$$

Again the sum of this series has to be split into the sum of the first terms + the sum of the second terms.

The series for the first terms is the same as previously.

The series for the second terms can be rewritten as follows:—

$$\left.\begin{matrix} CIRD^2 \\ CIRD^3 \end{matrix}\right\} \quad = \quad CIR(1 + D)D^2$$

$$\left.\begin{matrix} 2CIRD^4 \\ 2CIRD^5 \end{matrix}\right\} \quad = 2CIR(1 + D)D^4$$

$$\left.\begin{matrix} 3CIRD^6 \\ 3CIRD^7 \end{matrix}\right\} \quad = 3CIR(1 + D)D^6$$

which equals $CIR(1 + D)[D^2 + 2D^4 + 3D^6 + \ldots]$

If we now make $D^2 = x$ the series in the brackets [   ] becomes

$$x + 2x^2 + 3x^3$$

which is the same series as in Proof 2.

If the sum of the series $x + 2x^2 + 3x^3 + \ldots = \dfrac{x}{(1 - x)^2}$

the sum of the series $D^2 + 2D^4 + 3D^6 = \dfrac{D^2}{(1 - D^2)^2}$

$\therefore$ The sum of the second terms is $CIR(1 + D)\dfrac{D^2}{(1 - D^2)^2}$

and the sum of the whole original series is

$$\frac{C}{(1-D)} + \frac{D^2 CIR(1+D)}{(1-D^2)^2}$$

4. Proof that if the average gestation period for investment was such that sacrifice of consumption in year 0 provided no additional output until the beginning of year 2, instead of year 1, with the same pattern recurring in the future, then to achieve the same overall contribution to growth in the economy the social rate of return on investment in the two year gestation case, R', would have to be $\frac{(1+D)}{D}$ times as large as in the one year gestation case.

It has already been proved that ΣB for one year R equals

$$\frac{C}{(1-D)} + \frac{CIRD}{(1-D^2)}$$

and for two years R, or R' it equals

$$\frac{C}{(1-D)} + \frac{D^2 CIR'(1+D)}{(1-D^2)^2}$$

The condition to be satisfied now is that these two values of ΣB should be made equal

i.e. that $\quad \dfrac{C}{(1-D)} + \dfrac{CIRD}{(1-D)^2} = \dfrac{C}{(1-D)} + \dfrac{D^2 CIR'(1+D)}{(1-D^2)^2}$

i.e., $\quad \dfrac{R}{(1-D)^2} = \dfrac{D(1+D)R'}{D(1-D^2)^2}$

Now $\quad (1-D^2)^2 = (1+D)^2 (1-D)^2$

i.e. $\quad \dfrac{R}{(1-D)^2} = \dfrac{D(1+D)R'}{(1-D)^2(1+D)^2}$

i.e. $\quad R = \dfrac{DR'}{(1+D)}$

i.e. $\quad R' = \dfrac{R(1+D)}{D}$

5. Proof that investment with any social rate of return produces a smaller flow of benefit the longer its gestation period is. Specifically the ratio between the flows of benefit from an investment with a one year gestation period and one of the same size and with the same social rate of return once it is on stream, but when all the investment is made in year 0 and no output arises from it until the beginnings of years 2, 3 and n are as follows:—

Year investment comes on stream	Ratio
1	1
2	$\dfrac{D}{(1 + D)}$
3	$\dfrac{D^2}{1 + D + D^2}$
n	$\dfrac{D^{n-1}}{1 + D + D^2 + \ldots + D^{n-1}}$

In view of the complication of this subject it may help to restate the definitions which it is proposed that we should use:—

R — The actual average social rate of return on investment in the economy assuming that the average gestation period for investment is one year.

Potential R — The potential average social rate of return on investment in the economy · assuming that the average gestation period for investment is one year and that demand conditions are optimum.

R' — The actual average social rate of return on investment in the economy assuming that the average gestation period for investment is not one year.

r — The potential social rate of return from a particular quantum of investment with a one year gestation period.

r' — The potential social rate of return from a particular quantum of investment of the same size as previously with a gestation period differing from one year, but with a flow of benefit of equal magnitude to that provided by investment with a one year gestation period and social rate of return r.

We are now not concerned with the whole economy but with a given quantum of resources devoted to particular investments. When these investments come on stream it is assumed that their social rates of return will be divided between I and C in the same ratio as for all other output in the economy. It is also assumed that the part of the extra output which is reinvested will have the same characteristics in terms of social rates of return and pay off period as the first quantum. In other words we are concerned with investment of particular characteristics which are likely to repeat themselves through time. This is a fair assumption because very rarely are industries built up only to be run down again very quickly afterwards as a matter of policy.

With a given quantum of investment, which we can make equal to unity let us consider the benefit from it in terms of the future flow of consumption which it will produce with all the usual assumptions. Let us make the sum of these flows of benefit equal to $\Sigma B'$.

The flow of benefit for $\Sigma B'$ is in fact the same as the second terms for the normal summations for ΣB, i.e. for a one year maturity period.

$$\Sigma B' = CIrD$$
$$+ 2CIrD^2$$
$$+ 3CIrD^3$$
$$+ \ldots$$

From previous summations we know that the value of this series is

$$\frac{CIrD}{(1-D)^2} \text{ (Proof 2)}$$

For a two year gestation period, by analogy with Proof 3 the value of the sum of the series for $\Sigma B'$ is

$$\frac{D^2 CIr'(1+D)}{(1-D^2)^2}$$

and again by analogy it can be seen that

$$r' = r\frac{(1+D)}{D}$$

— if the value for $\Sigma B'$ is going to be the same in each case.

Let us now consider the case where investment, all undertaken in year 0 produces no output until the beginning of year 3 with the same process repeated in the future. The value for $\Sigma B'$ are now

$$
\left.
\begin{array}{lll}
\text{Year 1} & \text{nil} \\
\text{Year 2} & \text{nil} \\
\text{Year 3} & CIr'D^3 \\
\text{Year 4} & CIr'D^4 \\
\text{Year 5} & CIr'D^5 \\
\text{Year 6} & 2CIr'D^6 \\
\text{Year 7} & 2CIr'D^7 \\
\text{Year 8} & 2CIRD^8
\end{array}
\right\}
\begin{array}{l}
= CIr'D^3(1 + D + D^2) \\
\\
+ \\
\\
= 2CIr'D^6(1 + D + D^2)
\end{array}
$$

Again by analogy with Proof 3 it can be seen that the sum of this series for $\Sigma B'$ is

$$
\frac{D^3 CIr'(1 + D + D^2)}{(1 - D^3)^2}
$$

Putting this value of $\Sigma B'$ equal to the one for the one year gestation period we get

$$
\frac{CIrD}{(1 - D)^2} = \frac{D^3 CIr'(1 + D + D^2)}{(1 - D^3)^2}
$$

simplifying and expanding the bottom terms on the right hand side we get

$$
\frac{r}{(1 - D)^2} = \frac{D^2 r'(1 + D + D^2)}{(1 - D)^2(1 + D + D^2)^2}
$$

$$
r = \frac{D^2 r'}{(1 + D + D^2)}
$$

$$
r' = \frac{r(1 + D + D^2)}{D^2}
$$

From this it can be seen how the pattern develops as n, the number of years till pay off starts, gets larger.

There are three stages which follow the same sequence in each case, whatever the value of n

1. The series for $\Sigma B'$ take the form

$$
\begin{aligned}
\Sigma B' = &\; CIr'D^n \;(1 + D + \ldots + D^{n-1}) \\
&+ 2CIr'D^{2n}(1 + D + \ldots + D^{n-1}) \\
&+ \ldots
\end{aligned}
$$

2. The sum of the series for $\Sigma B'$ takes the form

$$
\frac{D^n CIr'(1 + D + D^3 + \ldots + D^{n-1})}{(1 - D^n)^2}
$$

3. When the one year and n year values of ΣB are made equal they always simplify the same way.

In particular $(1 - D^n)^2 = (1 - D)^2 (1 + D + D^2 + \ldots + D^{n-1})$ for any value of n.

The general case for the relationship between r and r' for investment which comes on stream at the beginning of year n, with all the sacrifice of consumption being made in the year 0 is therefore

$$r' = r \frac{(1 + D + D^2 + \ldots + D^{n-1})}{D^{n-1}}$$

The sum of the series $1 + D + D^2 + \ldots + D^{n-1}$ from Proof 1 is

$$\frac{1 - D^n}{1 - D}$$

The only difference between this expression and the one in Proof 1 being that in this case the value of D^n is not tending to zero because n is a finite number.

$$\therefore r' = r \frac{r(1 - D^n)}{D^{n-1}(1 - D)}$$

Now what has been shown so far is that as gestation periods lengthen so the value of r' has to rise to produce the same flow of benefit as investment with a one year gestation period. It can also be seen that in every case the value for $\Sigma B'$ is in exact ratio to the value of r or r'.

It follows from this that if the social rate of return on investment with a gestation period of more than one year is not r' but r then the value of the flow of benefit which results is $\Sigma B' \times \dfrac{r}{r'}$. Let this equal $\Sigma B''$.

We now have $\Sigma B'' = \Sigma B' \times \dfrac{r}{r'}$

or
$$\frac{\Sigma B''}{\Sigma B'} = \frac{r}{r'}$$

i.e. the flow of benefit from an investment all made in year 0 which comes on stream at the beginning of year n is r/r' times the flow of benefit which would have been produced if the gestation period was one year, i.e. for investment coming on stream at the beginning of:

Year 1   the ratio is 1

Year 2   the ratio is $\dfrac{D}{(1 + D)}$

Year n the ratio is $\dfrac{D^{n-1}}{(1 + D + D^2 + \ldots + D^{n-1})}$ or $\dfrac{D^{n-1}(1 - D)}{(1 - D^n)}$

6. Proof that investment with any social rate of return tends to produce a much more substantial flow of benefit if its gestation period is very short. Specifically the ratio between the flows of benefit from an investment with a one year gestation period and one of the same size and with the same social rate of return but a gestation period of less than one year is very closely approximate to:—

$$\frac{12}{\text{gestation period measured in months}}$$

Let us start by considering a quantum of investment with a social rate of return r' such that the flow of benefit from this investment, which in this case takes less than a year to mature, exactly equals the flow of benefit from another quantum of investment the same size, with a social rate of return r which does take one year to mature.

Again we are not now concerned with the whole economy but with a given quantum of resources devoted to particular investments. When these investments come on stream it is assumed that their social rates of return will be divided between I and C in the same ratio as for all the other output in the economy. It is also assumed that the part of the extra output which is reinvested will have the same characteristics in terms of social rates of return and pay off period as the first quantum. In other words we are again concerned with investment of particular characteristics which repeat themselves over time.

Let us assume that the quantum of investment we are considering has a gestation period of m months, such that m divides evenly into 12. It will be seen later that this assumption can be relaxed without the result being invalidated.

When considering the flow of benefit from the quantum of investment we are considering let us, as a first approximation, assume that any flow of benefit in year 0 does not have to be discounted because of D, and that all benefit in year 1 has to be multiplied by D, in year 2 by D^2, etc.

As with Proof 5, let us now consider the series of values for $\Sigma B'$ resulting from in this case our short gestation period quantum of investment.

The values for year 0 are as follows:—

$$\frac{m}{12} \cdot CIr'$$

$$+ \frac{m}{12} \cdot 2CIr'$$

$$+ \ldots$$

$$+ \frac{m}{12} \cdot \frac{(12 - m)}{m} CIr'$$

The reason why each term is prefaced by $m/12$ is that this is the length of time when the flow of benefit measure by terms in CIr' is current before the size of the benefit flow alters. The reason why the last term is $(12 - m)/m$ and not $12/m$ is that the benefit from investment is only received in the period after it is carried out so that there will be m months at the beginning of the year with no benefit from this quantum of investment and hence $(12 - m)$ months when the benefit is obtained.

Similarly the values of $\Sigma B'$ for year 1 are as follows:—

$$\frac{m}{12} \cdot \frac{12}{m} CIr'D$$

$$+ \frac{m}{12} \cdot \left(\frac{12}{m} + 1 \right) CIr'D$$

$$+ \ldots$$

$$+ \frac{m}{12} \cdot \left(\frac{24 - m}{m} \right) CIr'D$$

The terms of the series for $\Sigma B'$ can now be laid out as follows

$$\text{Year } 0 - \frac{m}{12} \cdot CIr' \left[1 + 2 + \ldots + \frac{12 - m}{m} \right]$$

$$\text{Year } 1 - \frac{m}{12} \cdot CIr'D \left[\frac{12}{m} + \left(\frac{12 + 1}{m} \right) + \left(\frac{12}{m} + 2 \right) + \ldots + 24 - m \right]$$

$$= \frac{m}{12} \cdot CIr'D \left[1 + 2 + \ldots + \frac{(12 - m)}{m} \right] + \frac{m}{12} \times \frac{12}{m} \times \frac{12}{m} CIr'D$$

$$\text{Year } 2 - \frac{m}{12} \cdot CIr'D^2 \left[1 + 2 + \ldots + \frac{(12 - m)}{m} \right] + \frac{12}{m} CIr'D^2$$

$$\text{Year } n - \frac{m}{12} \cdot CIr'D^n \left[1 + 2 + \ldots + \frac{(12 - m)}{m} \right] + \frac{12}{m} CIr'D^n$$

Now the value of the sum of the terms in the square brackets is obtained from the standard formula for summing an arithmetic series, viz.

$$\frac{\text{First term} + \text{Last term}}{2} \times \text{number of terms}$$

As the number of terms in the square brackets is $\frac{(12 - m)}{m}$ the sum of

the terms in the square brackets is

$$\frac{1 + \frac{(12 - m)}{m}}{2} \times \frac{(12 - m)}{m} = \frac{(m + 12 - m)(12 - m)}{2m^2}$$

$$= \frac{6(12 - m)}{m^2}$$

$$\therefore \Sigma B' = CIr' \times \frac{6(12 - m)}{m^2} \times \frac{m}{12} \left[1 + D + D^2 + \ldots + D^n \right]$$

$$+ \frac{12}{m} CIr' \left[D + 2D^2 + \ldots + nD^n \right]$$

The value of the series for $[1 + D + D^2 + \ldots + D^n]$ is found from Proof 1 — and for $[D + 2D^2 + \ldots + nD^n]$ from Proof 2

$$\therefore \quad \Sigma B' = CIr' \left[\frac{(12 - m)}{2m} \times \frac{1}{(1 - D)} + \frac{12}{m} \times \frac{D}{(1 - D)^2} \right]$$

$$= CIr' \left[\frac{(12 - m)(1 - D) + 24D}{2m(1 - D)^2} \right]$$

Now $\Sigma B'$ for the same quantum of investment with a one year gestation period and social rate of return r, with the same benefit flow is as follows

$$\Sigma B' = \frac{CIrD}{(1 - D)^2}$$

Making these two expressions equal and solving for r' in terms of r we get

$$CIr' \left[-\frac{(12-m)(1-D)+24D}{2m(1-D)^2} \right] = \frac{CIrD}{(1-D)^2}$$

$$\therefore \qquad r' = r \left[\frac{2mD}{12 - 12D - m + mD + 24D} \right]$$

$$= r \left[\frac{2mD}{(12 + 12D) - (m - mD)} \right]$$

Now whatever values of m and D are chosen within any reasonable bounds the value of $(m - mD)$ is going to be small in relation to $(12 + 12D)$. Furthermore it also is going to make the bottom line of the squared bracket closer to the value of $(12D + 12D)$ than $(12 + 12D)$ which it is at the moment.

As a close first approximation let us assume that it has exactly this effect.

We now have $r' = r \dfrac{2mD}{12D + 12D}$

$$r' = r \times \frac{m}{12}$$

By exactly the same line of argument as at the end of Proof 5, it follows that the flow of benefit from a quantum of investment with social rate of return r and not r' and gestation period m months is the reciprocal of the relationship between r and r'

i.e. $\dfrac{12}{m}$

It is also quite clear that this general relationship does not depend on m being divisible into 12 without a remainder.

7. Proof that the ratios between the flows of benefit from an investment with a one year gestation period and one of the same size but with the outlay spread evenly over more than one year before it comes on stream are as follows

Year investment
comes on stream   *Ratio*

1

$$1 = \frac{1}{1} \times \frac{(1-D)}{D} \left[\frac{D}{(1-D)} \right]$$

2

$$\frac{1}{2} \frac{(1-D)}{D} \left[\frac{D}{(1-D)} + \frac{D^2}{(1-D^2)} \right]$$

3

$$\frac{1}{3} \frac{(1-D)}{D} \left[\frac{D}{(1-D)} + \frac{D^2}{(1-D^2)} + \frac{D^3}{(1-D^3)} \right]$$

n

$$\frac{1}{n} \frac{(1-D)}{D} \left[\frac{D}{(1-D)} + \frac{D^2}{(1-D^2)} + \ldots + \frac{D^n}{(1-D^n)} \right]$$

Yet again we are not now concerned with the whole economy but with a given quantum of resources devoted to particular investments. When these investments come on stream it is assumed that these social rates of return will be divided between I and C in the same ratio as for all the other output in the economy. It is also assumed that the part of the extra output which is reinvested will have the same characteristics in terms of social rates of return and pay off period as the first quantum. In other words again we are concerned with investments of particular characteristics which repeat themselves over time.

Let us consider first the flow benefit from a quantum of investment spread equally over a two year period, years 0 and 1, and which comes on stream at the beginning of year 2, and compare it to the flow of benefit which would arise from the same quantum of investment if it were all deployed in year 1 assuming the same social rate of return.

Let the flow of benefit from the investment all made in year 1 be $\Sigma B'$ and from the investment spread equally over years 0 and 1 be $\Sigma B''$

Now since that half of the investment made in year 1, in the two year case, has the same gestation period as in the one case the flow of benefit from this half is subject to no reduction in value because of its gestation period compared with the one year case, though of course it is half the size.

Furthermore we already know from Proof 5 what the reduction in benefit flow will be from that half of the investment made in year 0 which does not come on stream till year 2; it is in the ratio $1 : \frac{D}{(1+D)}$

The relationship between $\Sigma B'$ and $\Sigma B''$ is therefore as follows:—

$$\Sigma B'' = \frac{1}{2}\Sigma B' + \frac{1}{2}\Sigma B' \frac{D}{(1+D)}$$

i.e.

$$\frac{\Sigma B''}{\Sigma B'} = \frac{1}{2}\left[1 + \frac{D}{(1+D)}\right]$$

By an exactly analogous process it can be seen that the ratio between $\Sigma B''$ and $\Sigma B'$ for a three year case would be

$$\Sigma B'' = \frac{1}{3}\Sigma B' + \frac{1}{3}\Sigma B' \frac{D}{(1+D)} + \frac{1}{3}\Sigma B' \frac{D^2}{(1+D+D^2)}$$

$$\therefore \qquad \frac{\Sigma B''}{\Sigma B'} = \frac{1}{3}\left[1 + \frac{D}{(1+D)} + \frac{D^2}{(1+D+D^2)}\right]$$

From this it can be seen that in the general case for an n year gestation period the ratio between $\Sigma B''$ and $\Sigma B'$ would be

$$\frac{\Sigma B''}{\Sigma B'} = \frac{1}{n}\left[1 + \frac{D}{(1+D)}\right.$$
$$\left. + \frac{D^2}{(1+D+D^2)} + \ldots + \frac{D^{n-1}}{(1+D+D^2+\ldots+D^{n-1})}\right]$$

If we now multiply the whole expression by $(1-D)$ and divide each term in the brackets by $(1-D)$ we obtain

$$\frac{\Sigma B''}{\Sigma B'} = \frac{1}{n}(1-D)\left[\frac{1}{(1-D)} + \frac{D}{(1-D)(1+D)} + \frac{D^2}{(1-D)(1+D+D^2)}\right.$$
$$\left. + \ldots + \ldots \frac{D^{n-1}}{(1-D)(1+D+\ldots+D^{n-1})}\right]$$

Now from Proof 5 we know that terms of the form

$$(1-D)(1+D+D^2+\ldots+D^{n-1}) = (1-D^n)$$

$$\therefore \quad \frac{\Sigma B''}{\Sigma B'} = \frac{1}{n}(1-D)\left[\frac{1}{(1-D)} + \frac{D}{(1-D^2)} + \frac{D^2}{(1-D^3)} + \ldots + \frac{D^{n-1}}{(1-D^n)}\right]$$

To make each term in the brackets concerned with the same power of D, let us now divide the whole expression by D and multiply each term inside the square brackets by D. We now get

$$\frac{\Sigma B''}{\Sigma B'} = \frac{1}{n}\frac{(1-D)}{D}\left[\frac{D}{(1-D)} + \frac{D^2}{(1-D^2)} + \frac{D^3}{(1-D^3)} + \ldots + \frac{D^n}{(1-D^n)}\right]$$

This being the general term the values for 1, 2, 3 and n year outlays are shown to be as laid out at the beginning of this Proof.

There is one final point to be made which relates to Proofs 5 and 7. In Chapter II, when Welfare Analysis was being developed, there was an underlying assumption that there was no material change in the income level of the community between the time when consumption was foregone for investment and the time when the gestation period for this investment was completed. This is a reasonable assumption in the case of investment with a gestation period of a year or two, but it ceases to be reasonable with very long gestation periods, particularly if the economy is growing rapidly so that the difference in standard of living at the beginning of the gestation period is materially lower than at the end. This would lend to a situation where consumption were being foregone at a relatively low standard of living to produce output not only much later but at a time when standards of living were considerably higher. In these circumstances factor d could clearly not be ignored and would make the flow of benefit from investment with long gestation periods even lower than Proofs 5 and 7 indicate.

Appendix B

The procedure adopted in the text for assessing the increase in benefit resulting from any particular rate of growth has a great virtue of comparative simplicity, but is open to criticism on the grounds that it is unsatisfactory to use a function which involves linear relationships for one year and logarithmic ones subsequently. There are two different arguments involved here. One is that the procedure proposed involves an acceptable degree of approximation leading to inconsistency, and the other is that it is conceptually unsound. The approximation argument would be sustainable if it could be shown that choosing different rates of growth produced different ratios between income and benefit, but this point can be disposed of by reference to Table B.1 which shows that the errors involved here are very small even if the future is discounted to a small extent, and become very small indeed if reasonable rates of discount of the future are allowed for. The argument that the approach adopted is conceptually unsound rests on the proposition that a different result is obtained for the values for total benefit and optimum savings ratios if the flow of benefit which we are considering year after year is obtained by taking logarithms of the consumption involved each year and then adding them together. However this approach is itself open to grave objections. The main problem is that having taken the logarithms of the various consumption levels for different years, it is entirely illegitimate to use normal procedures for adding logarithms together to find total benefit, because adding logarithms is tantamount to multiplying their antilogs and we are not concerned with multiplying together the benefit from different years' consumption but with adding them up. The only possible way through this problem might be to obtain some actual values for all the logarithms and then add these together without using any of the inappropriate summing procedures. However, this task would be fraught with difficulties involving negative values and arbitrary constants, and in any case is quite unnecessary because we already know that the difference between the values of the logarithms of consumption for consecutive years is going to be the same, since there is the same proportionate increase in consumption every year. All that remains to be done is to make the assumption, which is proved in the

Table B.1

Cumulative Growth Rate p.a.	2½%	5%	10%	% error Between 2½% & 10% Growth Rates
Income Level Year 0 →	100	100	100	
Income level after respective number of years producing identical increases in benefit measured on linear/ log scale				
4 , 2 , 1	110.3	110.3	110.0	.3%
8 , 4 , 2	121.8	121.6	121.0	.7%
12 , 6 , 3	134.5	134.0	133.1	1.1%
16 , 8 , 4	148.5	147.7	146.4	1.4%
20 , 10 , 5	163.9	162.9	161.1	1.7%
24 , 12 , 6	180.9	179.6	177.2	2.1%
28 , 14 , 7	199.6	198.0	194.9	2.4%
32 , 16 , 8	220.4	218.3	214.4	2.8%
36 , 18 , 9	243.2	240.7	235.8	3.1%
40 , 20 , 10	268.5	265.3	259.4	3.5%

Basis for Calculating Table:– Comparison of Terms $(1.025)^4$ $(1.025)^8$ etc. with $(1.05)^2$, $(1.05)^4$ etc. and $(1.10)^1$, $(1.10)^2$ etc.

It will be noted that the rate of divergence shown in the last column is far lower than any rate of discount of the future which it is reasonable to accept. Allowing for discounting the future, values of benefit are reduced by their distance away in time much more rapidly than they rise due to growth in consumption. Thus the total error involved in the linear/log procedure adopted is very small indeed.

text not to be a strong one, that, over small changes of income, benefit is proportional to income, and we are then left with only a simple summation with the result being directly related to the actual benefit being obtained this year. We can thus conclude that the procedure used in the text relating benefit this year to benefit in the future is internally consistent within very narrow limits, and that there is no reason to believe that the results obtained from it are suspect because they conflict with those obtained from a method of using logarithms which is inappropriate in the circumstances.

Notes

Chapter I

1. This list of commitments follows those in an article by Prof. Kaldor in the *Economic Journal*, March 1971.
2. National Accounts of O.E.C.D. Countries 1953-69.
3. *Annual Abstract of Statistics* (H.M.S.O.) various years between 1950 and 1970).
4. National Accounts of O.E.C.D. Countries 1953-69.
5. National Accounts of O.E.C.D. Countries 1953-69.
6. Samuel Brittan makes this important point in *Steering the Economy* (Penguin, 1971) p. 16 and elsewhere.

Chapter II

1. According to conventional economy theory, the social rate of return would equal the private rate if there were perfect competition in all markets, constant returns to scale, no external economics and no taxation. The rate of return on capital would then equal its marginal product, and everything would be in equilibrium. The approach adopted in this book does not regard this type of analysis as very helpful because the real world is so different from the theoretical one that the conditions posited are never attained. The social rate of return is always likely to differ from the private rate. If they are the same this is likely to be a coincidence.
2. This section draws heavily on the discussion of the declining marginal utility of income in *The Uneasy Case for Progressive Taxation* by Blum and Kalven (University of Chicago Press, 1966.)
3. *Aspiration and Affluence* by Katona *et al.* (McGraw Hill N.Y. 1971 p. 172 *et seq.*)
4. Quoted in Blum and Kalven *op. cit.* p. 63.
5. Katona *et al. op. cit.* p. 129.
6. *Critique of Welfare Economics* by I. M. D. Little (Oxford University Press, 2nd Edn. 1957, p. 34). The other proposals for direct measurement of the

declining marginal utility of income are taken from Blum and Kalven *op. cit.* p. 56 *et seq.*

7. Especially Pigou and Harrod, although Blum and Kalven do not find their arguments convincing (*op. cit.* p. 47).

8. More strictly we are assuming $\dfrac{dR}{dI} = 0$.

9. Figures are from *Annual Abstract of Statistics* (H.M.S.O.)

10. Katona *et al. op. cit* p. 99

11. Katona *et al. op. cit.* p. 161 *et seq.*

12. The social rate of return on education is dealt with *in extenso* in an article by Blaug in *The Economics of Education* by I. M. Blaug (Ed.) (Penguin Mod. Econs. 1968).

13. Mr. Walter Eltis pointed out this distinction in conversation.

14. These figures are estimates.

15. Much of the material in this section is based on *The British Economy in 1975* by Beckerman and Associates (Cambridge University Press, 1965) particularly Chapter VIII and IX.

16. The alternative assumption regarding Britain, whose savings ratio is well below the optimum figure shown in the tables and below that of almost every other country in the developed world, is that the rate of time preference in Britain is different from elsewhere. However, this argument is intrinsically implausible and is not supported by any empirical evidence — see Katona *et al. op. cit.* p. 179 *et seq.* The low savings ratio in Britain is much more easily explained by institutional factors than by unusual psychological attitudes.

17. Beckerman *op. cit.* Chapter III.

18. Particularly South Africa, Canada and Australia.

19. *1970 Annual Abstract of Statistics* (H.M.S.O.) p. 243. Table 265 shows export prices rising 11.4% between 1967 and 1969 and import prices 15.6%. However between 1965 and 1969 export prices rose 16.5% and import prices by 17.8% — a change in the terms of trade of 1.1% over the four period spanning the 1967 devaluation.

20. *A Manual of Applied Economics* by Prest *et al.* (Weidenfeld & Nicolson, 1970) pp. 228 *et seq.* has a discussion on income distribution on which this section has drawn heavily.

21. *Assessing Economic Performance* by Lipton (Staples Press, 1968) pp. 74 and 75.

22. Lipton *op. cit.* p. 57.

23. Though not with very high rates of inflation and long gaps between wage increases which involve substantial reductions in standards of living during the periods between wage increases as prices rise.

24. During the period 1954-1969 the average annual increase in price levels in Japan was 4.0%, the average for all O.E.C.D. countries was 3.0%, and the figure for the U.K. was 3.4%. (National Accounts O.E.C.D. Countries)

25. I am very grateful to Mr Eltis who drew my attention in conversation to the loss of current benefit resulting from under-utilised capital resources.

26. At least in the short term, although it is argued in Chapter IV that the social services in Britain have a desperate need for more resources to meet higher expectations, whose frustration leads to social distress.

27. This capital/output ratio is adjusted to allow for varying labour inputs. See the beginning of Chapter III.

28. The converse clearly is not true either. We have recently seen higher unemployment associated with more inflation.

29. See Chapter III for a detailed discussion of this point.
30. See particularly *Modern Economic Growth* by Kuznets (Yale University Press, 1966), pp. 220–234.

Chapter III

1. *Annual Abstract of Statistics* – various tables.
2. See figures already quoted in Chapter II note 19.
3. *Annual abstract of Statistics* – various tables.
4. *National Income and Expenditure Blue Book* (H.M.S.O) – various tables.
5. *1970 Annual Abstract of Statistics* Table 265 p. 243.
6. The Harrod-Domar growth models imply a relationship of this sort. More recently Prof. J. R. Sargent has taken this view, e.g. in his article 'Recent Growth Experience in the Economy of the U.K.' in *Economic Journal*, March 1968.
7. Prof. W. Beckerman certainly takes this view in *The British Economy in 1975* (Cambridge University Press 1975), particularly in Chapter VIII.
8. The descriptions of policy changes in this table are taken almost word for word from Samuel Brittan's *Steering the Economy* (Penguin, 1971). I am most grateful to him for permission to incorporate this material into the text here.
9. The high unemployment in the U.S.A. biases the average upwards. Most of continental Europe enjoyed very low unemployment indeed during the period under review.
10. National Accounts of O.E.C.D. Countries p. 171.
11. National Account of O.E.C.D. Countries p. 84
12. Beckerman *op. cit.* especially Chapter VIII.
13. I am grateful to Mr. Terry Pitt who drew my attention to this point.
14. The change in the terms of trade over the four years 1965–1969 spanning the 1967 devaluation was 1.1%. See note 19 to Chapter II.
15. During nearly all years since World War II the profits post tax and depreciation of manufacturing industry in Britain have been larger than the value of new investment undertaken.
16. These figures are taken from 'Inflation in Post-War Britain' by Dicks-Mireaux in *Inflation* by Ball and Doyle (Penguin, 1969).
17. The total value of what are normally referred to as the 'Sterling Balances' is approximately £3,500m.
18. It is important to note that the conclusions which follow are not strongly dependent on the utility function employed in Chapter II.
19. Particularly Britain, although the U.S. is another case in point.
20. See, for example, *The Economics of Europe* by John Pinder (Ed.) (Charles Knight & Co. Ltd. London, 1971) especially p. 14.
21. It has been estimated that the costs of the Anglo-French partnership led to the total costs being 25%–30% higher than they would have been if one country only had been involved. The delay factor is more difficult to quantify but must be substantial, though it is, of course, arguable that development by either country on its own would have taken even longer – though this would have depended on political decisions. For detailed arguments see *The Concorde Affair* by John Davies (Leslie Frewin, London 1969).
22. Almost all our merchandise exports to E.E.C. Countries are semi-manufactured or manufactured products which are fairly price elastic. Our imports

from the E.E.C., on the other hand, comprise a substantial element of foods which are not very price sensitive at the moment and which become effectively even less so under the C.A.P. provisions.

23. These figures are obtained from consideration of the White Paper and estimates produced by Prof. Kaldor published in the *New Statesman* 1971 in a series of articles, especially during March and July.

Chapter IV

1. John Pinder, *op. cit.* p. 14, states that from Britain joining the Common Market 'the best estimate is a welfare gain of 1% of GNP by 1978, declining to ¾% of GNP by 1980 and rising again thereafter'. This is a very small increase considering the huge changes involved, and is of such small magnitude over such a long period as to be liable to be swamped by the margins of error involved. For example, nowhere in *The Economics of Europe* is there any systematic discussion of the impact of demand changes caused by joining the E.E.C. on our growth prospects. By contrast the New Policy proposals in this book posit a welfare increase, worked out on the same basis as Mr. Pinder's, of about 15% in 5 years. On the Welfare Analysis scale developed in this book, the difference is much wider still.

2. John Pinder, *op. cit.*, is a notable exception to this statement, but the thoroughness of the analysis in his book is all too rare. Unfortunately, as already mentioned, the supposed gains turn out to be very small and rely on what is argued in this book to be much too static an approach to the problem in hand. In particular, far too little attention is paid to the implications of our joining the Common Market on the pressure of demand we are likely to be able to sustain during the coming years.

3. As Sir Roy Harrod pointed out in *Towards a New Economic Policy* (Manchester University Press. 1967) p. 2.

4. This point is made by Lipton *op. cit.* p. 78.

5. Katona *et al. op. cit.* p. 93 and elsewhere.

Index